PAUL SELIGSON
TOM ABRAHAM
CRIS GONTOW

2nd edition

English ID

Workbook
3

ID Language map

		Question syllabus	Vocabulary	Grammar	Speaking & Skills
1	1.1	Do you know all your classmates?		Questions with prepositions	Answer questions about yourself
	1.2	How do couples meet?	Relationships Phrasal verbs		Compare well-known love stories
	1.3	How many Facebook friends do you have?	Types of friend	Prepositions	Answer a quiz about someone you're attracted to
	1.4	Do you have many social media profiles?	Personality adjectives	Emphatic forms	Give opinions about social media
	1.5	How much time do you spend online?	Active listening phrases		Listen & order the story of Antony & Cleopatra
2	2.1	How green are you?	Going green		Answer questions about green habits
	2.2	How long have you been studying here?	Time / frequency / degree phrases	Present perfect continuous	
	2.3	How has the climate been changing?	The environment	Present perfect vs. Present perfect continuous	Ask & answer about personal habits
	2.4	What's the best ad you've seen recently?		Simple past vs. Present perfect / continuous	Talk about your work experience
	2.5	Do you support any charities?	Endangered species Expressions of percentage		Talk about endangered species
3	3.1	Which city would you most like to visit?	Cities	*a / the*	Describe your hometown
	3.2	Was your last vacation as much fun as you'd hoped?	Social conventions	Past perfect	Write a review
	3.3	Do you ever want to get away from it all?	Urban problems		Talk about the problems in your city
	3.4	Have you ever missed any important dates?		Past perfect continuous vs. Past perfect	
	3.5	Do you always follow the rules?	Sign phrases		Listen & make rules
4	4.1	Does your school system work well?	School subjects *do / get / make / take* collocations		Talk about school subjects
	4.2	What's the ideal age to go to college?	School problems	*too / enough*	Talk about jokes in English
	4.3	What do you regret not having done?		*Should have* + participle	Talk about regrets
	4.4	What would you do if you won a million dollars?		First & second conditional	Use conditional sentences
	4.5	What makes someone a genius?		*a / an / the* Third conditional	Sympathize & criticize
5	5.1	Are you a shopaholic?	Shopping & technology		Share shopping experiences
	5.2	What shouldn't you have spent money on?	Loans		Talk about shopping habits
	5.3	Have you ever borrowed money from a relative?		Modals of possibility / probability	Express surprise
	5.4	Have you ever bought a useless product?	Word formation	Order of adjectives	
	5.5	Do you often buy things on impulse?	Shopping		

		Question syllabus	Vocabulary	Grammar	Speaking & Skills
6	6.1	What are you watching these days?	TV genres & expressions Compound nouns	Prepositions	Talk about TV preferences
	6.2	What's your favorite TV show ever?		Relative Clauses 1 *a / an / the*	Ask & answer about TV preferences
	6.3	What was the last movie you saw?		Relative Clauses 2	
	6.4	Where do you usually watch movies?	Movies		Talk about surprising personal information
	6.5	Who are the wildest celebrities you know?			Talk about celebrities
7	7.1	Does technology rule your life?	Technology phrases		
	7.2	What was the last little lie you told?	*say* vs. *tell*	Reported Speech 1	Talk about the worst lie you've told
	7.3	How much of your day is screen time?		Indirect questions	
	7.4	Are machines with personality a good idea?		Reported Speech 2	Report requests & commands
	7.5	How often do you use a pen?	Activities		Talk about time spent on social media
8	8.1	How important are looks?			Talk about fake video technology
	8.2	Do you like watching illusions?		Modal perfects – *must have, can't have, may / might have*	Talk about street performances
	8.3	Have you ever cut your own hair?	*have* vs. *get*	Causative form	Talk about the things you do & the things you get done
	8.4	Do you have a lot of furniture in your room?	Furniture	Tag questions	Record a description of your house or apartment
	8.5	What's the hardest part of language learning?	Word formation		Write a comment about your listening skills
9	9.1	Does crime worry you?	Crime & violence	Review of verb families	Talk about famous crimes in your country
	9.2	How could your city be improved?		Passive voice	Talk about what makes you proud of your city
	9.3	Have you ever been to court?	Crime & punishment	Prepositions	Talk about yourself
	9.4	Where will you be living ten years from now?	Staying safe online *by*	Future perfect / continuous	Talk about how you stay safe on social media
	9.5	Do you watch TV crime dramas?	Excuse phrases		
10	10.1	What drives you crazy?		Binomials	Share your favorite love, hate, or anger quote
	10.2	What do you love to hate?	Pet hates	Gerunds	Talk about a pet hate
	10.3	How assertive are you?		Verb + gerund or infinitive Tense review	
	10.4	How similar are you to your friends?	Phrasal verbs	Separable & inseparable phrasal verbs Reflexive pronouns	
	10.5	What do you find hardest about English?			Talk about your strengths & weaknesses in English

Audio script p. 54   Answer key p. 64   Phrasebank p. 70   Wordlist p. 76   Verbs p. 78

1.1 Do you know all your classmates?

1 Match speed-friending events 1–3 to people a–g.

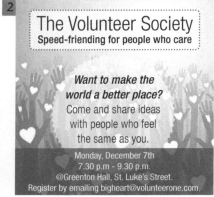

a ☐ I've just moved into the East End.
b ☐ I just hate the silly, superficial small talk typical of speed-friending.
c ☐ I'm a language student, and I love parties.
d ☐ I'm free on September 28th.
e ☐ My friends and I do volunteer work for a couple of charities when we can.
f ☐ Cooking is something I'm really good at.
g ☐ It's three weeks to Xmas. I don't want to spend the holidays alone.

2 Order the words in a–g to form questions. Be careful, there's one extra word in each.
a Facebook / have / do / How / you / you / many / friends / ?
b most / Who / do / makes / laugh / you / ?
c at / you / What / good / on / are / really / ?
d nervous / What / you / makes / are / ?
e last / did / do / does / What / vacation / you / ?
f speed-friending / Would / go / like / you / to / to / event / a / to / ?
g just / without / do / something / What's / live / you / can't / ?

3 Match questions a–g from **2** to these answers.
1 My cell phone, for sure.
2 Yes, I think they look fun.
3 I went to a water park with my cousins. We had a great time.
4 First dates. I never know what to say!
5 Reading and writing. I'm not very good at speaking or listening.
6 I have no idea! Too many to remember, that's for sure.
7 My friend Jack. He's such a funny guy.

4 🎧 **Make it personal** ▶ 1.1 Listen to the questions and answer using these words.

| first dates | tablet | sports |
| friend | mom | tests |

a What's something you just can't live without?
Well, let's see …
b What are you good at?
That's a difficult one. Er …
c What makes you nervous?
That's a good question. Well …
d Who are you closer to, your mom or your dad?
Hmm, let me think …
e What's the most fun place you've been to?
Hmm, I'm not sure …

1.2 How do couples meet?

1 Three authors made notes for a love story. Complete the notes with one word in each gap.

Love Story 1	Love Story 2	Love Story 3
They meet.	• They met.	They start hanging _____.
They fall _____ love.	• They got _____ really well.	She falls _____ him.
They _____ engaged.	• They fell _____ each other.	They move _____ together.
They get married.	• _____ _____ engaged.	He'll cheat _____ her.
They drift _____.	• They _____ married.	They'll break _____.
They get divorced.	• They lived happily ever after.	They'll get _____ together.

2 Match the stories in **1** to their views: a, b, or c.

a A fairy tale. b A boomerang relationship. c An extinguished candle.

3 Read the summary of *Romeo and Juliet*. Number the events in the correct order, 1–9.

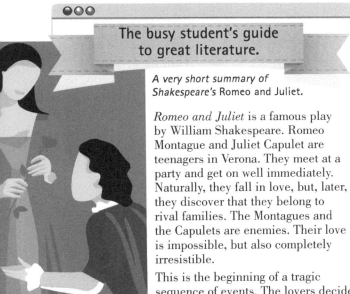

The busy student's guide to great literature.

A very short summary of Shakespeare's *Romeo and Juliet*.

Romeo and Juliet is a famous play by William Shakespeare. Romeo Montague and Juliet Capulet are teenagers in Verona. They meet at a party and get on well immediately. Naturally, they fall in love, but, later, they discover that they belong to rival families. The Montagues and the Capulets are enemies. Their love is impossible, but also completely irresistible.

This is the beginning of a tragic sequence of events. The lovers decide to escape with help from a friar. The friar marries them secretly, but they can't stay together. Romeo is exiled from Verona. The friar has a plan. He gives Juliet a herbal drink. She will "sleep" for 42 hours, enough for everyone to think she is dead. Then they will get together and leave Verona. Sadly, Romeo hears about Juliet's death, but doesn't know about the plan. He can't live without Juliet. He buys some poison, finds Juliet, and kills himself. Juliet wakes up and, finding Romeo dead, she takes his dagger and kills herself too. This classic romance has been an inspiration for generations of authors since.

4 ▶1.2 Listen to the summary of *Romeo and Juliet* without reading. Check how much you understood.
☐ 10–20% ☐ 30–50% ☐ 60–80% ☐ 90–100%

5 ▶1.3 Look at the sound picture for the schwa, /ə/. Listen and repeat the sound and the words.

6 ▶1.4 Listen to extracts a–d and underline the schwas in each line. The number is in parentheses.
a They meet at a party and get along well immediately. (4)
b Their love is impossible but also irresistible. (2)
c The friar marries them secretly. (4)
d ... but they can't stay together. (2)

7 **Make it personal** Find a simple summary of a well-known love story online. Exchange links with a study buddy and decide which you both prefer.

☐ Romeo dies
☐ escape
☐ meet
☐ Juliet dies
☐ get married secretly
☐ find out their families are enemies
☐ fall for each other
☐ get along well
☐ realize their love is impossible

1.3 How many Facebook friends do you have?

1 ▶ 1.5 Order the words in italics to complete definitions a–d. Listen to check.
   a Acquaintances generally aren't *can / on / count / people / you /*.
   b Friends are *usually / people / are / in / with / contact / you /*.
   c Good friends are *along / people / get / with / you / and / hang / out / with /*.
   d Very close friends are *always / rely / people / can / on / you / the /*.

2 ▶ 1.6 Listen to a podcast about National UnFriend Day. What is it?

3 ▶ 1.6 Listen again. According to the podcast, which two things define a true friend? Someone who ...
   ☐ is on your Facebook.
   ☐ helps you move house.
   ☐ shares his / her routine with you.
   ☐ has seen you recently.
   ☐ asks curious questions about you.
   ☐ is very good and nice.

4 Complete the Facebook comments.

Liz Hunter posted a photo
Friendship turned into love.
Mum and Dad at school in 1985.

Bethany Greer
Great photo, Liz. How long have they been married?

Liz Hunter
25 years! Mum had a crush ____ Dad from day one.

Lou Webster
My parents used to hang ____ with yours, Lizzie!

Liz Hunter
I know, Lou. My dad and yours got ____ well.

Lou Webster
Yeah! My dad borrowed money ____ yours, but never paid it back!

John Webster
My son doesn't know what he's talking ____. I'll deal ____ you when you get home tonight, Lou!

Liz Hunter
LOL!

5 ▶ 1.7 Listen to a–f and check the correct column, acquaintances (A), friends (F), or very close friends (V).

	A	F	V
a Tom and Lucy			
b Ben and Lou			
c J J and Bill			
d Sue and Rob			
e Joe and Pete			
f Meg and Amy			

6 **Make it personal** Think of someone you're attracted to and do the quiz. Write yes (Y) or no (N) in the first box.

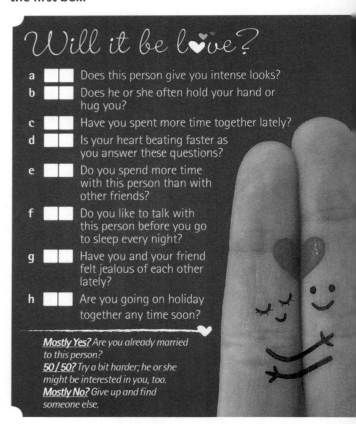

Will it be love?

a ☐☐ Does this person give you intense looks?
b ☐☐ Does he or she often hold your hand or hug you?
c ☐☐ Have you spent more time together lately?
d ☐☐ Is your heart beating faster as you answer these questions?
e ☐☐ Do you spend more time with this person than with other friends?
f ☐☐ Do you like to talk with this person before you go to sleep every night?
g ☐☐ Have you and your friend felt jealous of each other lately?
h ☐☐ Are you going on holiday together any time soon?

Mostly Yes? Are you already married to this person?
50 / 50? Try a bit harder; he or she might be interested in you, too.
Mostly No? Give up and find someone else.

7 ▶ 1.8 Listen to Gwen doing the quiz. Check / Cross her answers in the second box. What should she do?

8 **Connect**
Create a quiz with questions about you. Email it to a friend and find out how well they know you.

1.4 Do you have many social media profiles?

1. Match words 1–10 with words / suffixes a–h to make personality adjectives.

   1 adventure
   2 easy
   3 fun
   4 knowledge
   5 like
   6 open
   7 out
   8 self
   9 soc
   10 thought

   a minded
   b loving
   c seeking
   d ful
   e iable
   f going
   g able
   h centered

2. Look at the selfies. Which adjectives from **1** can you use to describe each person? More than one adjective might be possible.

   adventure-seeking   easygoing   fun-loving
   knowledgeable   like-minded   open-minded
   outgoing   self-centered   sociable   thoughtful

3. ▶ 1.9 Complete Chloe and Jake's conversation about people to follow on social media with emphatic forms of the words in parentheses. Listen to check.

   Jake: Oh, look at him. He looks quite boring and self-centered.
   Chloe: Yes, that one _____ not for me. (**definitely / be**)
   Jake: What about this one? They _____ very sociable. (**sure / look**)
   Chloe: Yes, they look fun. And I _____ people who are a bit silly. I'll follow them. (**like**)
   Jake: Ah, look at this one. What a cute couple.
   Chloe: Hmm, yes they _____ in love. (**certainly / be**) But they're a bit over the top, don't you think? I _____ it when people are like that. (**hate**)
   Jake: Ha! Yes, I know what you mean!

4. ▶ 1.10 Listen and copy the stress and intonation in extracts a–e.

5. Match questions 1–5 to opinions a–e.
   1 What's important to you in a friend?
   2 What do you think about people who post lots of selfies on social media?
   3 Do you think we use social media too much?
   4 What's the best social media app? Why?
   5 How can you stay safe online?

   a I do believe we use it a lot, but I don't think it's a problem.
   b It's definitely important not to share too much information about yourself.
   c I do think we should be like-minded.
   d They sure are self-centered, but I don't mind. I like posting them myself.
   e I don't know. I like them all!

6. 🎤 **Make it personal** ▶ 1.11 Listen to check and email your opinion to your teacher.

1.5 How much time do you spend online?

1 People a–j have met through a dating service. Read and decide what each person wants after their first date.

a Jerry about Wang: "I had a good time with Wang. We both like *Star Trek* movies, but that's not enough for me."
b Wang about Jerry: "Jerry's such a charming guy. I hope he'll ask me out again."
c Zoe about Joe: "Joe is the most handsome guy I've ever met. He's totally gorgeous!"
d Joe about Zoe: "Zoe is great! I'd love to date her."
e Bernie about Lilly: "Lilly and I just didn't click at all."
f Lilly about Bernie: "Bernie and I didn't get along. Scientific matching isn't perfect after all."
g Marney about Ben: "Ben and I had fabulous chemistry for a blind date! He could be the one!"
h Ben about Marney: "I can't wait to see Marney again. She's such fun, but only as a friend, sadly."
i Hannah about Caleb: "Well, he is fun to be with, I guess, but there was no attraction between us."
j Caleb about Hannah: "It was a little embarrassing. She's great, but not the one for me."

2 ▶1.12 Classify italic words in a–h: noun (N), adjective (ADJ), adverb (ADV), or verb (V). Listen and copy the stress and intonation.
a Montagues and Capulets were *rival* families. ADJ
b Romeo and Juliet fell for each other *immediately* when they met. ____
c Romeo and Juliet's was an *impossible* love. ____
d Good *communication* is essential in both friendship and love. ____
e The hardest thing about marriage is learning to *communicate* with each other. ____
f When Jo and I met, there was instant mutual *attraction* between us. ____
g *Respect* is the most important thing in any relationship if it's going to last. ____
h I got a divorce because my ex didn't *respect* me at all. And he was cheating on me, too. ____

3 ▶1.13 Listen and order the story of Antony and Cleopatra, 1–6.

4 ▶1.14 Follow the model. React to the stories you hear.

So, Antony is married to Flavia.

You mean Fulvia, right?

a You mean Fulvia, right?
b No way! With Cleopatra, right?
c So what happens next?
d Hang on a sec! He marries Caesar's sister?
e Are you serious? He cheats on her, too?
f And then?
g Whoa! What a crazy story!

Can you remember ...
▶ 3 verb forms for the present? SB→p. 7
▶ 6 phrasal verbs for relationships? SB→p. 8
▶ 6 compound adjectives for personality? SB→p. 12
▶ when auxiliary verbs are stressed? SB→p. 13
▶ 10 personality adjectives? SB→p. 13

2.1 How green are you?

1 Read the start of the article and check the correct meaning of "go off the grid".
- [ ] not use regular electricity
- [ ] ride a bike (cycle)
- [ ] turn the lights off

Pedal! For how long?
Physics teacher John Cornell's classroom at Henleigh High School will "go off the grid" for a day this Friday. But that does not mean they can't use any electrical items. Instead, there'll be pedal power to generate electricity.

2 Read the rest of the article. True (T) or False (F)? Correct the false statements.

Cornell and another teacher connected a bike to a power generator two weeks ago. As students pedal, their energy is converted into electricity that is stored in a car battery in the classroom.
"Students have been coming into our classroom an hour before class and staying for another hour after school to power the generator by cycling", Cornell said. When the battery's full, the students will vote for what they want to use the electricity for. Students will then calculate how much energy they'll need to do whatever they want to do.
For example, to watch a movie, they'll need to cycle for 72 minutes in order to power the TV and DVD player. To make waffles, they'll need much more energy and more pedaling. "This project is great fun and we've learned a lot," a student commented. "To get electricity you have to do hard work. I unplug my laptop and cell phone charger when I'm not using them now," another confirmed.

a Cornell is a chemistry teacher who started this idea on his own.
b The generator and battery are in different rooms.
c Students have been generating electricity on their own time.
d The teacher tells them how much energy each item needs.
e Watching a movie in class uses more energy than powering a waffle maker.
f At least one of John's students has learned to be greener.

3 Add one word to complete comments a–g. Are the speakers green (G) or not green (NG)?
a Yeah! We won't use plastic cups in this office anymore.
b What? Three thousand dollars for couple of solar panels? Forget it!
c Can have a couple more plastic bags, please?
d It's pretty simple be eco-friendly. I just try to reuse, reduce, and recycle.
e What? Recycling? It's useless. Forget!
f Are you joking? Why take the stairs when you can take elevator?
g I work in same office as my neighbor, Bill. Sometimes he drives me; other days I drive him.

4 ▶ 2.1 Match a–g in 3 to replies 1–7. Listen to check.
1 Yes, but you will save a lot more money than that on electricity bills.
2 I'm so glad. Those cups take 500 years to decompose.
3 I know. The three Rs. But it's not so easy!
4 No, it isn't. Think of all the trash you create when you throw things away.
5 Can I join you? That'd make it cheaper for the three of us.
6 Because the exercise is good for you and it will save energy.
7 Here you are. Would you like to buy a reusable bag?

5 Complete the sentences with a word from box 1 and a suffix from box 2.

1	2
energy fuel pet recharge reuse	able efficient friendly

a This product is _____, so it won't harm your dog.
b Let's get an _____ light bulb to put in that lamp.
c Hybrid cars are more _____ than traditional cars.
d Can I get a _____ bag for my groceries, please?
e It's got a _____ battery, you just need to remember to charge it!

6 Order the words to form green survey questions.
a plastic / home / you / do / recycle / at / ?
   Do you recycle plastic at home?
b flexitarianism / practice / you / ever / do / ?
c you / have / home / energy-efficient / light bulbs / do / at / ?
d transportation / using / of / you / to / walked / have / or cycled / work / lately / instead / private / ?
e when / appliances / using / you're / you / do / turn off / not / them / ?
f use / do / you / eco-friendly / products / cleaning / ?
g have / plastic / reusable / changed / from / you / to / cloth bags / ?

7 ▶ 2.2 Match a–d to the responses. Find four examples of /ɑ/ or /oʊ/ in each pair. Listen to check.

a Is the hotel down the road open?
b Don't go alone. I'll come with you.
c Has John gone to the vet?
d Hey, that's a nice orange top!

- [ ] Yeah. His dog stopped eating.
- [ ] Thanks a lot. I got it at the new store.
- [ ] Yes, I think so.
- [ ] Great! Get your coat.

8 🎤 **Make it personal** Record your answers to the questions in **6**, then share them with a classmate.

9

2.2 How long have you been studying here?

1 Amir made a list of "green" resolutions on January 1st. Use the notes to complete his blog with the present perfect continuous + or –. There is one extra note.

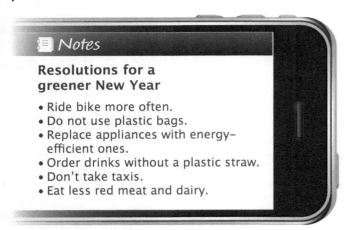

Notes

Resolutions for a greener New Year
- Ride bike more often.
- Do not use plastic bags.
- Replace appliances with energy-efficient ones.
- Order drinks without a plastic straw.
- Don't take taxis.
- Eat less red meat and dairy.

posts about contact

June 30th

I've been trying to go green for the last six months. It hasn't been easy, but I feel truly proud of myself. So far, I've managed to change quite a few things for the better. So, first of all ¹<u>I've been bike riding</u> to work twice a week. The exercise is good for me and I feel a lot healthier now, but it isn't much fun when it's windy and worse when it rains! 😞 And also on transportation, ² _____ . It makes it hard to get home at night, but I'm saving a lot of money.

I'm shopping differently at the moment, too. ³_____, because this type of plastic isn't recyclable and is filling up our seas, damaging the wildlife. Instead I take my own reusable bag. In cafés and restaurants, ⁴_____, too. It's unnecessary and produces so much plastic waste. ⁵_____, too, because raising cattle isn't very environment-friendly and uses up lots of the earth's valuable resources. I don't really miss it much to be honest, and I'm eating a lot more healthy now.

2 Reread and answer a–f.
a How does Amir feel about his achievement? ¹
b What's the disadvantage of cycling to work?
c What's the advantage of not taking taxis?
d What problems does using plastic create?
e How does he feel eating less red meat and dairy?
f Does Amir's blog encourage you to do the same?

3 ▶ 2.3 Many countries have been going green lately. Read changes a–h and predict which country is doing each. Listen to check.

| Austria | Brazil | Costa Rica | France |
| Iceland | Norway | Sweden | Switzerland |

a In _____, architects have been building energy-efficient houses.
b _____ has been using clean electricity from geothermal energy.
c _____ has been building national Alpine parks.
d _____ has been planting millions of trees to reduce deforestation.
e _____ has been using more water and wind power for electricity.
f _____ has been collaborating with Sweden to produce clean energy.
g _____ has been producing a lot of its fuel from sugar cane.
h In _____, more families have been installing solar panels at home.

4 Correct two mistakes in each of a–g.
a The office have been really busy. We've been worked like crazy.
b I like your shoes. I've been trying find a pair like that last year.
c So sorry! Have you been waited for a long?
d Hey! I've been trying to call you yesterday. Where was you?
e He's been studied English for year.
f They've been playing the soccer before.
g Joan been managing the company advertising since 2012.

5 ▶ 2.4 Make sentences with the present perfect continuous. Follow the model.

Model: *Try to call you.*
You: *I've been trying to call you.*

6 🎤 **Make it personal** What have you done this year to be "green"? Make a list of things you've done.

7 📡 **Connect**
Use your phone to record your answers and share them with a classmate.

2.3 How has the climate been changing?

1 Order the letters to spell environment phrases.

a NGIAOPCH
b RDUGOHTS
c OSLDFO
d NSEDROFATOIET
e NGIRSI ESA VLEESL
f PNGIUDM FO EESTWA
g TNHERTDEAE PCEISES
h LFSOSI LSEFU
i MEATLIC NECAGH

2 ▶2.5 Listen to two students and check the four problems in **1** they mention.

3 ▶2.5 Listen again and answer a–f.
a Does their city suffer from floods or droughts?
b Were Lucy and Mikaela personally affected?
c Have the authorities repaired all of the damage?
d When was the last time it rained in the north?
e What percentage of the earth is water?
f Which country does Lucy give as an example?

4 ▶2.6 Imagine significant progress is made in the next 50 years to protect the environment. Read the future news, and write the verbs in the present perfect or perfect continuous. Listen to check.

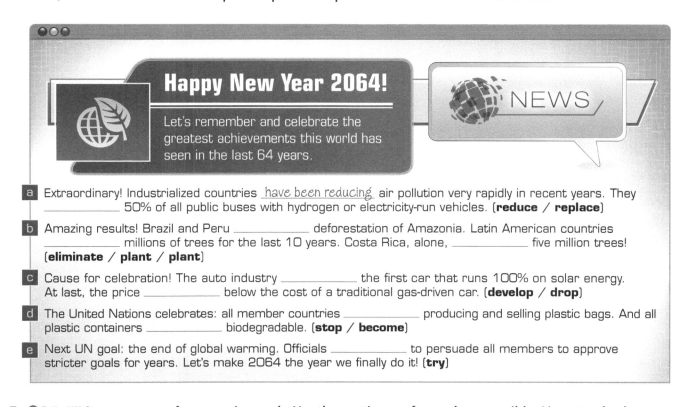

a Extraordinary! Industrialized countries _have been reducing_ air pollution very rapidly in recent years. They _____ 50% of all public buses with hydrogen or electricity-run vehicles. (**reduce / replace**)

b Amazing results! Brazil and Peru _____ deforestation of Amazonia. Latin American countries _____ millions of trees for the last 10 years. Costa Rica, alone, _____ five million trees! (**eliminate / plant / plant**)

c Cause for celebration! The auto industry _____ the first car that runs 100% on solar energy. At last, the price _____ below the cost of a traditional gas-driven car. (**develop / drop**)

d The United Nations celebrates: all member countries _____ producing and selling plastic bags. And all plastic containers _____ biodegradable. (**stop / become**)

e Next UN goal: the end of global warming. Officials _____ to persuade all members to approve stricter goals for years. Let's make 2064 the year we finally do it! (**try**)

5 ▶2.7 Write present perfect questions a–h. Use the continuous form where possible. Listen to check.
a How long / you / know / your best friend?
b You / work hard / recently?
c You / ever / live / in a different city?
d How long / you / study / today?
e How much bread / you / eat / today?
f How far / you / walk / today?
g How many cups of coffee / you / drink / today?
h You / exercise / a lot / lately?

6 🎧 **Make it personal** Share your answers to **5** with a classmate. Any surprises?

11

2.4 What's the best ad you've seen recently?

1 Read and match pop-up adverts 1–5 to Internet users a–e.
   a I'm a qualified young woman with no previous experience. I need to get a job fast.
   b We're soccer fans and we're tired of adverts on TV.
   c I'm a senior manager working for a multinational company. I am looking for an agent who can help me manage my career.
   d I'm a sales representative for a large consumer goods company that hopes to export to Asian countries.
   e I'm a Mac user with a slow, slow laptop. Get me out of here!

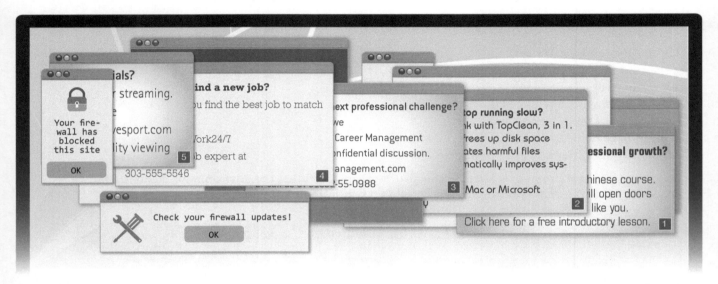

2 ▶ 2.8 Predict and write the words you can't see. Listen to check. Would you contact any of these companies?

3 Add the missing words to make complete questions.
   a Ready for professional growth?
   b Laptop running slow?
   c Looking for your next professional challenge?
   d Want to find a new job?
   e Tired of commercials?

4 ▶ 2.9 Listen to three calls to the companies in 1 and answer a–f. Mia (M), Cal (C), or Jake (J)?
   Which caller ...
   a has not contacted the company before?
   b has never met a representative of the company before?
   c has been waiting the longest?
   d received a guarantee?
   e leaves contact details?
   f currently has no work?

5 ▶ 2.9 Complete extracts a–f with the correct form of the verbs in parentheses. Listen again to check.
   a I _____ in for an interview a couple of weeks ago. (**come**)
   b It _____ two weeks and I _____ anything from you. (**be / not hear**)
   c Hello. You _____ the offices of Grabowsky and Loewe. (**reach**)
   d I _____ in the oil industry for 17 years now. (**work**)
   e I _____ a copy of Selling in China for Beginners and, er, it _____ yet. (**order / not arrive**)
   f I _____ my bank account and I _____ five weeks ago, so I _____ for 35 days. (**check / pay / wait**)

6 Correct the mistake in each sentence.
   a I've started this course in February.
   b I've been having my job for five years.
   c Our teacher has given us lots of homework last week.
   d I've been learning 10 new words this lesson.
   e I haven't gone out last night.

7 **Make it personal** Which of the sentences in 6 are true for you? Change the others so they're true.

2.5 Do you support any charities?

1 ▶ 2.10 Listen to four dialogues and identify the animals mentioned in each.

> Giant panda   Golden lion tamarin   Monk seal   Ivory-billed woodpecker
> Javanese rhino   Mountain gorilla   North Atlantic right whale

2 ▶ 2.11 These extracts are in phonetics. Can you decipher them? Listen to check and notice the /ə/.
  a /aɪm gəʊɪŋ tə teɪk ə fəʊtəgræf/
  b /aɪ kən siː ðæt ðeɪ ə(r) iːtɪŋ fruːt/
  c /hələʊ ənd welkəm tə zuː ətlæntə/
  d /mʌðə(r) ənd tʃaɪld trævəlɪŋ əlɒŋ/

3 ▶ 2.12 Order the words in a–e to form questions. Cross out the extra word in each. Listen, check, and answer.
  a animal / you / have / ever / endangered / a / seen / an / in / wild / the / ?
  b a / you / have / a / ever / one / seen / in / zoo / ?
  c animal / sick / looked / on / have / after / you / ever / a / ?
  d given / never / have / you / an / money / for / animal / ever / cause / ?
  e NGO / an / have / ever / considered / you / it / working / for / animal / protection / ?

4 Read the charity ad and change the underlined expressions to percentages (%).

A third of all our food depends on bees and other insects pollinating the plants it grows from.

The number of bees in Europe has fallen drastically in recent years, and now *a tenth* of bees face extinction.

Because of intense farming over the last century, *hardly any* of their natural environments now remain.

5 ▶ 2.13 *Dictation*. Listen and complete a–e with four or five words each. Encouragement (E) or discouragement (D)?
  a _____ you'll get there.
  b _____ doing that?
  c Keep going. You'll _____ .
  d _____ succeed, try, try again.
  e Do you really think _____ ?

6 ▶ 2.14 Listen to two short dialogues and check the phrases in **5** that you hear. What does each person want to do?

7 🎤 Make it personal Which of the animals in this lesson would you adopt (i.e., give money to a charity to save)?

Can you remember ...
▸ 7 "green" adjectives using -able, -efficient, and -friendly? SB→p.19
▸ 3 words that rhyme with *go* and 3 that rhyme with *hot*? SB→p.19
▸ 4 frequency expressions, 4 quantity expressions, and 8 time expressions? SB→p.21
▸ 9 environmental disasters / problems? SB→p.22
▸ 2 differences between the present perfect and the present perfect continuous? SB→p.23
▸ 7 species of animals we may never see again? SB→p.26
▸ 3 encouragement and 3 discouragement expressions? SB→p.27

3.1 Which city would you most like to visit?

1 Use the clues to complete the crossword with adjectives to describe cities.

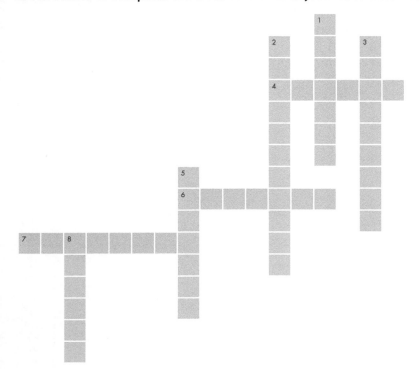

Across:
4 When the air is dirty with a mixture of smoke and fog.
6 An area of a city where people with a lot of money live.
7 When the air / sea is dirty from traffic and industry.

Down:
1 When everything is very busy and confusing.
2 An area of the city where lots of people want to live.
3 An area which hasn't had much care or maintenance.
5 An area in a very bad state.
8 An area which is busy and where people have fun.

2 Complete the sentences with words from **1**.
a I live in a _____ neighborhood. Everyone wants to live there.
b This used to be a nice part of town, but nowadays it's looking _____ because most of the buildings are old and damaged.
c After an accident at the chemical factory, the river became very _____ .
d Have you tried driving in the downtown area? It's _____!
e In rush hour there's a lot of traffic so the air becomes very _____ .
f If you want to have fun, go to Lapa. It's a really _____ part of the city.

3 ▶3.1 Order the words in a–d. Complete the answers with *a* or *the*. Listen to check. What city is it?
a you / like / city / how / your / do / ?
It's _____ truly awesome city; _____ city that never sleeps; _____ capital of _____ world.
b way / it / easy / is / to / your / around / find / ?
It is really easy to find your way around because _____ streets are numbered.
c your / what's / landmark / favorite / ?
Well, in _____ city of skyscrapers, I guess it's _____ Chrysler Building.
d spots / are / the / what / most / tourist / popular / ?
Central Park, Greenwich Village, 5th Avenue, _____ World Trade Center, and so many others.

4 ▶3.2 Listen and repeat. Pronounce the underlined sounds correctly.

It's a p<u>i</u>ty our pr<u>e</u>tty c<u>i</u>ty <u>i</u>s now l<u>i</u>ttered w<u>i</u>th l<u>i</u>ttle b<u>i</u>ts of plast<u>i</u>c.
/ɪ/

Three sl<u>ee</u>py sh<u>ee</u>p on a b<u>ea</u>ch, <u>ea</u>ch <u>ea</u>ting a p<u>ie</u>ce of gr<u>ee</u>n ch<u>ee</u>se.
/iː/

5 🎧 **Make it personal** Answer the questions from **3** for yourself. Share your answers with a classmate. Do you agree?

14

3.2 Was your last vacation as much fun as you'd hoped?

1 Chris is in Mumbai to meet his fiancée's family. He's arranged to meet a friend, Roni, first. Read Roni's texts and mark a–f True (T), False (F), or not mentioned (N).

> Finally made it to the hotel, but you'd left. Sorry! Good luck with your in-laws. R
> Sent 17:31

> Remember not to kiss your girlfriend in front of her parents. Terrible manners in India! R
> Sent 17:35

> Almost forgot. Hug her brothers if you want to, but don't kiss them on the cheek, OK? R
> Sent 17:42

> One more: don't greet servants as you do with the family. Just nod. Can u reply, pls? R
> Sent 17:45

> Aha! Can't see my texts 'cause u turned off your cell phone as I told you. ☹ R
> Sent 18:36

a By the time Roni got to the hotel, Chris had gone.
b Chris sent five texts to Roni.
c Roni had told Chris to turn his phone off while visiting his future in-laws.
d Chris told Roni that he had turned his phone off.
e Indian men don't greet other men with kisses.
f You're not supposed to shake hands with the servants.

2 Complete Chris' email to his family with the past perfect form of these verbs.

break	(not) hug	kiss	make
mistake	send	shake	tell

Dear Mom and Dad,
Greetings from a really rainy Mumbai—I thought it'd be hot and dry. Last night I met Diya's parents. After a tense couple of hours I got back to the hotel, turned my cell phone back on (Roni ᵃ_____ me to switch it off), and found several text messages with advice from Roni. Too late! He ᵇ_____ those messages while my phone was off. As I read them I realized I ᶜ_____ so many terrible mistakes at Diya's. To begin with, I had kissed her in front of her parents, apparently a big no-no in India. To make matters worse, I ᵈ_____ her brothers, too — males usually don't. Worse still, I ᵉ_____ them as you're supposed to. Worst of all, I ᶠ_____ one of the servants for a member of the family and ᵍ_____ hands with her. In India, you greet people from different social backgrounds differently. In other words, I discovered I ʰ_____ practically every cultural rule in the book. I just hope they'll give me another chance. Wish me luck! I'll write again soon. Hope Dad's feeling a little better now.
Love,
Chris xx

3 Correct one mistake in each of a–e.
a Did you know the Romans had spoken Latin?
b After we had arrived home, we made some sandwiches.
c By the time we got home, the TV show finished.
d When I had lunch, I had a short nap.
e We had bought our car five years ago.

4 Choose the correct past participle.
a Chris had been / gone by the time Roni arrived.
b Chris had never been / gone to Mumbai before.
c Roni had been / gone to India several times.
d By the time Chris saw Roni's messages, he'd already been / gone to his in-laws'.

5 ▶ 3.3 Watch / Listen to the host and underline the word(s) with the strongest stress in a–f. The number of stressed words is in parentheses.

a Hi, this is your travel host. (4)
b I'd like to show you the top ten attractions of Madrid, Spain. (8)
c Number ten, Plaza de Cibeles. Madrid is known for many beautiful squares like this one. (9)
d The Cibeles fountain is an important symbol of this city. (5)
e Number nine. Almudena Cathedral. It took more than a hundred years to complete its construction in 1993. (8)
f The original site was occupied by Madrid's first mosque. (6)

6 ▶ 3.4 Listen and copy the sentence stress.

7 🔴 **Make it personal** Write a short review of a hotel, restaurant, or attraction you know well. Share it with a friend. Do they agree?

3.3 Do you ever want to get away from it all?

1 Read comments from four people about where they live. Match the topics in the box to each person.

crime   driving   money   noise

Carlos
I've sold my car recently and now I only use public transportation. I hated it because I always got stuck in ¹_____ jams and could never find a parking ²_____ . Also, there's a lot of car ³_____ so I was always afraid I'd lose it one day.

Anya
There's a lot of ⁴_____ round here, you can see it everywhere, from broken windows to graffiti. There's also a lot of ⁵_____ on the buses, especially when it's crowded. It's a constant worry, you have to keep your hands on your bags and pockets to stop people stealing from you. The crime ⁶_____ in general is very high.

Mike
My city isn't a quiet place. People are always ⁷_____ their horns loudly, it makes me mad. Sometimes I just want to get away from all the ⁸_____ pollution and hide on a quiet beach forever!

Margaret
I live in a small town, where most of the young people have left to work in big cities. It's become very poor, and most people here are in ⁹_____ . They're struggling to pay their bills most of the time, so they don't have much of a work–life ¹⁰_____ .

2 Complete the comments in 1 with the words in the box. There are two extra words.

balance   debt   honking   noise
pickpocketing   rate   spot   construction
theft   trash   traffic   vandalism

3 Match phrases 1–10 to endings a–j to make phrases describing urban problems.

1 constantly   a loneliness
2 go through   b balance
3 suffer from   c parking spot
4 get stuck   d connected
5 find a   e theft
6 be in   f pollution
7 crime   g red lights
8 work–life   h in traffic jams
9 noise   i rate
10 car   j debt

4 Which of the urban problems do each of these sentences describe?
a Oh, no! Someone's stolen my car!
b I wish I had more friends, I hardly ever leave the house.
c I never get any free time any more. I just seem to work all the time.
d I don't know how I'm going to pay my bills this month.
e Uh-oh, it looks like the parking lot is full.
f You're never off your phone!

5 **Make it personal** Complete sentences a–c. Use words and phrases from this unit to help you. Then share your answers with a friend.
a I don't mind ..., but ... really annoys me.
b I wouldn't live in a city where / which ... .
c In big cities, it's difficult to ... .

3.4 Have you ever missed any important dates?

1 Complete the conversations with one word.
- a A: I was petrified watching that movie.
     B: No _____! It's a very scary movie.
- b A: We had a really good day in the end.
     B: Oh, yeah? How did it _____ out in the end?
- c A: I hate using taxis.
     B: What do you _____? I thought you used them all the time.
- d A: I had a nightmare at work today.
     B: You _____ thing! What happened?
- e A: That concert was boring.
     B: You're _____! I thought it was fantastic!

2 ▶3.5 Listen to problems a–g and match them to these sentences.
- ☐ He'd been locked out of the house.
- [a] He'd been stuck in a traffic jam.
- ☐ They'd been stuck in a subway train.
- ☐ They'd been stuck in an elevator.
- ☐ They'd been locked out of their car.
- ☐ They'd been stuck at the top of a building.
- ☐ They'd been stuck in a line for hours.

3 ▶3.6 What had they been doing? Listen, choose the correct verb, and write your guesses below.

| dance | do exercise | fight | fly | speed |

- a Bill and Jim _____.
- b Meg and her boyfriend _____.
- c Betty and Pete _____.
- d Joe and his girlfriend _____.
- e Suki _____.

4 Complete a–e with the verbs in parentheses in the past perfect or past perfect continuous.

- **a** Marge watched her husband come in and collapse on the couch. He _____ with his friends in the bar. (hang out)

- **b** As he walked through the door, he knew Wilma _____ his favorite brontosaurus rib pie. (make)

- **c** When Stan reached the top of the hill, he realized his friend _____ there a few minutes before. (get)

- **d** He was almost sick when he found out his roommate Leonard and his neighbor Penny _____ secretly for some time. (date)

- **e** In the end we find out that Severus Snape _____ Albus Dumbledore. (kill)

5 Two of sentences a–g are correct; the others have one mistake each. Correct them.
- a I had to sit down because I'd stood all day.
- b We got lost because we hadn't been understanding the directions.
- c Julio failed the exam because he hadn't studied enough.
- d Vera had been visiting Turkey before so she knew the best places.
- e Until yesterday night, I'd never been eating meat before.
- f Luigi only got married because he'd been living with his mother for 40 years.
- g How long were you waiting when the doors opened?

6 🔵 **Make it personal** Have you ever had any of the experiences in **5**? Tell a friend what happened.

17

3.5 Do you always follow the rules?

1 Match signs a–f to the places 1–6 you might see them.

a Speed limit 20 MPH
b Please do not distract the driver
c DEEP WATER—No swimming
d Strictly no parking!
e Please do not feed the animals
f No photography allowed

1 on a bus
2 at a zoo
3 at a lake
4 in an art gallery
5 on a street
6 in front of someone's house

2 Match the signs to phrases a–g and complete them with prepositions.

a Danger! No
b Kindly refrain
c Park here
d Please clean
e Tow
f Vehicles will be

_____ after your pet.
zone. Do not stop here.
towed _____ owner's expense.
your own risk.
lifeguard _____ duty.
_____ smoking.

3 ◯3.7 Listen to the sound effects and make rules with *can't* after the beep. Follow the model.

Excuse me. I'm afraid you can't take photos here.

4 ◯3.8 Match the two parts of the quotes. Listen to check.
a The golden rule is
b Life is short. Break the rules. Forgive quickly. Kiss slowly.
c Know the rules well,
d If you obey all the rules,
e You have to learn the rules of the game.
f There are three rules for writing a novel.

☐ Unfortunately no one knows what they are. Somerset Maugham
☐ so you can break them effectively. Dalai Lama XIV
☐ And then you have to play better than anyone else. Albert Einstein
☐ that there are no golden rules. George Bernard Shaw
☐ you miss all the fun. Katharine Hepburn
☐ Laugh uncontrollably. And never regret anything that makes you smile. Mark Twain

5 🎤 **Make it personal** Which of the quotes do you most agree with? Share your ideas with a classmate.

Can you remember ...
▶ 8 words for features of a city? SB→p.32
▶ 9 customs in Hong Kong? SB→p.34
▶ how to use the past perfect? SB→p.34
▶ 10 urban problems? SB→p.36
▶ 5 phrases to show you are listening? SB→p.38
▶ the difference between past perfect and past perfect continuous? SB→p.39
▶ 2 people, 4 verbs, and 4 preposition phrases from signs? SB→p.40

4.1 Does your school system work well?

1 Add vowels to the school subjects. Circle three /dʒ/ sounds and underline one /tʃ/.

L		T	R	T	R	
	R	T				
G		G	R		P	H	Y
M		T	H			
H		S	T		R	Y
L		N	G		G	S
C	H		M		S	T	R	Y
P	H	Y	S		C	S
B			L		G	Y

2 ▶ 4.1 Listen to two teachers. Who said it? Ruth (R) or Dan (D)?
a I think schools need to teach 21st century skills.
b I believe we should concentrate on reading, writing, and arithmetic.
c I think kids have to learn how to solve problems creatively.
d In my opinion, smart phones can be a useful learning tool in class.
e Smart phones shouldn't be allowed in class.
f I don't think students should look for information online. It's useless.
g Teachers should teach students to find information on the Internet that they can trust.

3 ▶ 4.2 Listen and match a–g in **2** to the agree / disagree responses.

Agree	Disagree
I think so, too.	I don't think so.
I completely agree with you.	I don't agree with you.
Yeah, you're right.	Oh, come on!

4 ▶ 4.3 Listen to the sentence stress. Then follow the model.

• • • •

Model: *I think so, too.*
You: *I think so, too.*

5 Complete the mind maps with these words.

> badly   a difference   an exam
> an exercise   feedback   good grades
> homework   into trouble   kicked out
> mistakes   photos   progress
> a report card   a test   well

Do

Get

Make

Take

6 Match 1–7 to a–g to make sentences. Underline the phrases you don't use a lot in English.
1 I haven't done
2 I'm under a lot of pressure to pass
3 Who would have guessed I'd get kicked
4 I know I should get a
5 The only way to do
6 It's really no secret that I must get
7 The career advisor told me it takes

a degree if I want to get a decent job.
b out of school for cheating on a test.
c excellent grades if I want to get a scholarship.
d over five years to train to be a vet.
e as well as I expected in school this year.
f my exams so I can get into college.
g well in school is to do homework and revise for tests.

7 🔴 Make it personal What subjects are / were you best / worst at? Why? Discuss with a classmate.

19

4.2 What's the ideal age to go to college?

1 Read a teacher's social media updates and circle the correct choice.

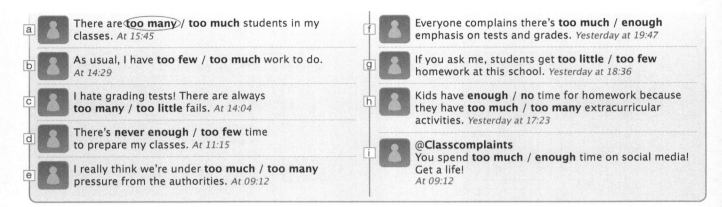

a There are **too many** / **too much** students in my classes. *At 15:45*

b As usual, I have **too few** / **too much** work to do. *At 14:29*

c I hate grading tests! There are always **too many** / **too little** fails. *At 14:04*

d There's **never enough** / **too few** time to prepare my classes. *At 11:15*

e I really think we're under **too much** / **too many** pressure from the authorities. *At 09:12*

f Everyone complains there's **too much** / **enough** emphasis on tests and grades. *Yesterday at 19:47*

g If you ask me, students get **too little** / **too few** homework at this school. *Yesterday at 18:36*

h Kids have **enough** / **no** time for homework because they have **too much** / **too many** extracurricular activities. *Yesterday at 17:23*

i @Classcomplaints
You spend **too much** / **enough** time on social media! Get a life! *At 09:12*

2 Cross out the wrong option in a–c.
a I haven't got enough **energy** / **money** / **rich** / **time** to …
b I've got too much **work** / **pressure** / **problems** / **stress** from …
c There are too many **distractions** / **noise** / **people** / **rules** at …

3 ▶ 4.4 Listen and repeat a and b. How fast can you go? Be careful to pronounce the /ʊ/ correctly every time.
a The woman could cook because she read the book.
b Hey! Look where you're putting your foot!

4 ▶ 4.5 Listen to a joke and circle the words you hear.

Three language students are **talking outside** / **walking to school** for their listening class.

"It's **Wednesday** / **windy**," says Yolanda.

"No, it isn't, it's **Thursday** / **thirsty**," says Jaime.

"Me, too," says Petra, "Forget class, let's find **a café** / **a coffee**!"

5 **Make it personal** What jokes do you know in English? Tell a classmate.

20

4.3 What do you regret not having done?

1 Look at the people in photos a–c. What do you think they regret?

2 Match what the people say to the photos in **1**.

1. I should have studied harder at school. I didn't take it seriously at the time, but now, doing this job, I realize how important it was.

2. I shouldn't have chosen political science as my major. I thought it would be interesting, but it isn't.

3. I shouldn't have gone out with my friends at the weekend. I should have studied for my test this morning.

3 Rewrite a–f as if you were regretting your choice.
   a "I didn't think carefully about my options."
      I should have thought more carefully about my options.
   b "Truth is I didn't get into law school 'cause I didn't work hard enough." I should have …
   c "Choosing engineering instead of art was a big mistake." I should have …
   d "Everybody says I didn't get the job because I didn't dress appropriately for the interview." I should have …
   e "My career just isn't taking off 'cause I didn't go to music school when I had the chance, I guess." I should have …
   f "I dropped out of college 'cause I wanted to make money straight away. Now I'm stuck in this boring, badly paid job." I shouldn't have …

4 ▶ 4.6 Listen and express regrets. Follow the model.

It was a mistake to drop out.

I shouldn't have dropped out.

5 ▶ 4.7 Order the phrases, 1–5, to make three dialogues a–c. Listen to check.
   a ☐ Really? What did you do?
      ☐ I was in 5th grade, I think, and I stuck the teacher's purse to a table.
      ☐ I have no idea. I really don't know.
      ☐ Why did you do such a thing?
      [1] I did something terrible at school once.
   b ☐ I looked my mother in the eye and told her that I hated her with all my heart.
      ☐ Really? What did you say?
      ☐ Yep! I don't really know where that came from.
      ☐ I said something really mean once.
      ☐ What a terrible thing to say!
   c ☐ So I hit it off with my hand, but it hit the wall and broke into a thousand pieces. And I realized it wasn't an insect. It was some kind of brooch.
      ☐ Oh, no! What a silly thing to do!
      ☐ I did the most embarrassing thing a while ago.
      ☐ This teacher came up to me and there was this insect on her blouse.
      ☐ Really? What did you do?

6 ▶ 4.8 Listen to extracts a–c, choose the correct option and react after the beep.

   a Really? What did you **say** / **do**?
   b Why would you **say** / **do** such a thing?
   c What a silly thing to **say** / **do**!

7 🗣 **Make it personal** Is there anything about your school life that you regret? Discuss with a classmate.

21

4.4 What would you do if you won a million dollars?

1 Aisha is a college student, majoring in technology. She's thinking about her future goals and aspirations. Match actions 1–6 to the results.

1 I'll probably graduate next year,
2 I think I'll move to San Francisco,
3 I might find a good job quickly,
4 I'd really like to travel the world,
5 I want a better computer
6 I have a big nose

a but it usually takes a long time.
b because I can't write very good apps.
c but I don't have enough money for tickets.
d and the first thing I'll do is look for a job with a tech company.
e and I hate it!
f it's a good place to find a tech job.

2 ▶ 4.9 Complete Aisha's goals and aspirations with the verbs. Listen to check and repeat.
   a If I graduate from college next year, I _____ a job with a tech company. (**look for**)
   b If I _____ to San Francisco, I'll find a good tech job. (**move**)
   c I _____ surprised if I find a good job quickly. (**be**)
   d If I _____ the lottery, I'd travel the world. (**win**)
   e I could write better apps if I _____ a better computer. (**have**)
   f If I _____ change one thing about myself, I'd have a smaller nose. (**can**)

3 Which of the sentences in exercise **2** are first conditional, and which are second?

4 ▶ 4.10 Match the words in **4** to the sound pictures. Listen to check.

blue	book	cook	could	moon
moved	pool	school	should
through	true	woman

5 🔲 **Make it personal** Write a first and second conditional sentence for each of the situations below.
   a Your national soccer team is in the semi-final of the World Cup. The team they're playing is very bad, but the team they'll play in the final is very good and it's unlikely they'll win.
   If my team wins the semi-final, they'll go to the final.
   If my team won the World Cup, …
   b You really want to buy a new car, but you don't have any money.
   _____
   _____
   _____
   c You live in a big house, but it needs some work.
   _____
   _____
   _____
   d You might go out this weekend.
   _____
   _____
   _____
   e You're thinking of becoming a politician.
   _____
   _____
   _____

4.5 What makes someone a genius?

1 ▶ 4.11 Read movie reviews 1–3 and complete them with *a*, *an*, or *the*. Listen to check.

Movie list #4: Geniuses

1 Gifted
Marc Webb directs __ movie about __ intellectually gifted seven-year-old girl and her uncle and grandmother's fight to have custody of her. The girl, Mary Adler, is played by __ actor Mckenna Grace, who gives __ outstanding performance. Mary lives with her uncle Frank, played by __ actor Chris Evans, but her grandmother wants to take her away and provide her with __ special tutor so as to exploit __ gift that she has. __ movie follows the battle between the uncle and the grandmother.

2 Magnus
Magnus is __ documentary movie by director Benjamin Ree, which follows __ fascinating journey of Magnus Carlsen to becoming chess grandmaster at __ age of 13. __ movie shows how __ strong interest in numbers when he was five years old led __ boy to become interested in chess, and his drive, devotion, and passion throughout __ journey.

3 Hidden Figures
Hidden Figures is __ biographical drama which tells __ incredible true story of three African–American women who worked at NASA in __ early 1960s. Each woman was __ brilliant mathematician and together they were __ brains who put astronaut John Glenn into space. __ story shows how __ women overcame strong gender and racial barriers and inspired many others.

2 Reread and answer a–d.
a How many actors are mentioned in the three reviews?
b Which movie(s) is / are about child geniuses?
c Which movie is about a legal battle?
d Which movie is about people who faced discrimination?

3 Order the words in a–g and write sympathy (S) or criticism (C).
a done / is / what's / done / .
b thinking / were / what / you / ?
c end / world / the / not / it's / the / of / .
d better / you / known / should've / .
e such / could / do / how / you / thing / a / ?
f you / get / let / don't / it / down / .
g you / will / learn / ever / ?

4 ▶ 4.12 Listen to problems 1–7 and react using expressions from **3**. Follow the model.
"I didn't get the scholarship because I didn't prepare for the interview."
Model: *g*
You: *Will you ever learn?*

5 ▶ 4.13 Complete the two sentences for each problem a–e. Listen to check.

a I didn't get the scholarship because I didn't prepare for the interview.
You (**should** / shouldn't) _____
If you ('**d** / hadn't) _____

b I failed the test because I didn't study.
You (**should** / **shouldn't**) _____.
If you ('**d** / **hadn't**) _____.

c I got really bad grades because I was absent a lot this semester.
You (**should** / **shouldn't**) _____.
If you ('**d** / **hadn't**) _____.

d I got kicked out of school because I cheated on a final exam.
You (**should** / **shouldn't**) _____.
If you ('**d** / **hadn't**) _____.

e My parents were upset because I couldn't get into college.
You (**should** / **shouldn't**) _____.
If you ('**d** / **hadn't**) _____.

6 🎤 **Make it personal** In pairs. Think about something you have done that you wish had been different. Share your experiences with a partner. Use expressions to show sympathy.

Can you remember ...

- 8 school words? SB→p.44
- 13 school subjects? SB→p.44
- 2 expressions with *do*, 2 with *get*, 1 with *make*, and 1 with *take*? SB→p.45
- how to use *too* and *enough* with adjectives? SB→p.46
- ⊕, ⊖, and ⊘ for *should have*? SB→p.48
- ⊕ and ⊖ for the first and second conditional? SB→p.51
- which syllable is stressed in three, four, or five-syllable words ending in -*y*? SB→p.52
- 4 phrases for sympathy and 4 for criticism? SB→p.53

23

5 5.1 Are you a shopaholic?

1 Read the advertisement and match three of the headings a–e to paragraphs 1–3.
   a You can cut costs.
   b You can expand your business.
   c You can use cutting-edge technology.
   d You can take time off.
   e You can get customers to your store.

Join us at Gen-Z Mall in 2020 and take your business into the future.

Coming in spring of 2020, the new Gen-Z Mall in downtown Austin will be the first of its kind. We are embracing the technology and shopping habits of Generation Z to bring you the best business possible. Here are three reasons why you should move your retail business here:

1 ____
We are providing ____ to all businesses and customers throughout and outside the mall, so everyone can access the Internet without paying. There will also be ____ throughout the mall so customers don't have to worry if their mobile devices lose power. We can also provide screens for ____ in clothing stores to save customers time and help them decide what clothes will look like before they buy.

2 ____
We've created a system where we provide ____ for customers to get special deals and discounts throughout the mall. These will only be valid if customers do ____ rather than buying online, though, so you can expect to see much more traffic into your business.

3 ____
We provide ____ terminals which will help you reduce staff costs while customers process their own purchases. We also actively encourage ____ by showing videos on large screens of products available in the mall. This will help you build ____ and so make sure your customers return.

2 Reread and complete with these words / phrases.

   brand loyalty   charging stations   coupons
   free Wi-Fi   self-checkout   in-store shopping
   virtual try-ons   user-generated content

3 Find 15 (3↘, 6→, 6↓) clothes and accessories in the word puzzle.

E	S	U	N	G	L	A	S	S	E	S
B	H	U	V	C	O	H	W	A	A	H
J	O	Z	I	O	U	C	E	V	R	O
K	R	F	Q	T	J	T	A	B	R	E
T	T	B	S	C	W	A	T	J	I	S
S	S	C	A	R	F	J	E	A	N	S
A	X	H	P	G	F	K	R	C	G	U
N	E	B	I	K	I	N	I	K	S	W
D	T	I	A	R	O	S	W	E	E	T
A	S	Y	N	E	T	A	A	T	R	T
L	J	E	W	E	L	R	Y	L	T	O
S	A	D	J	D	P	P	A	N	T	S

4 Which items from 3 complete phrases a–c?
   a I bought <u>a new pair of</u> ____ last week. (7 items)
   b I really want to buy <u>some</u> new ____. (8 items)
   c That's <u>a</u> nice ____. (7 items)

5 ▶5.1 Listen to six short phrases and write down the question you hear.

6 **Make it personal** Read the cartoon and think about your answers to the questions. Then share your ideas with a friend.

   a Do you ever compare prices online while you're in a store?
   b What types of things do you always / never buy online?
   c What's the best thing about buying things in-store?

5.2 What shouldn't you have spent money on?

1 **Complete the conversations with the missing prepositions.**
  1 A: Why do you look so happy?
    B: I've finally paid ... my loan!
  2 A: What did you do on the weekend?
    B: I went ... a shopping spree and bought lots of new clothes.
  3 A: Do you think you earn enough money in your job?
    B: Not really. I always run ... of money before the end of the month.
  4 A: It was hard financially, being a student. I had to take ... a loan.
    B: Me, too. In the end I got ... a lot of debt.

2 ▶5.2 **Listen to Jia and Andreas and answer the questions.**
  1 How much was the loan that Andreas applied for?
  2 How much does Andreas earn?
  3 Who agreed to help Andreas?
  4 How much interest will he pay?
  5 When is his first payment due?

3 ▶5.3 **Listen to extracts a–d and circle the word you hear.**
  a If I'd planned my application more carefully, they **would / might / could** have accepted it.
  b If I **hadn't / haven't / wouldn't** gone on vacation twice this year, I wouldn't have got into debt.
  c If you'd told me, I would **of / had / have** helped you.
  d So if she hadn't died, I **didn't / wouldn't / hadn't** have received it.

4 ▶5.4 **Listen and repeat a–d twice. Try to join the words together.**

5 ▶5.5 **Put the words in the columns. Listen to check.**

| bought | doubt | enough | fasten |
| laugh | listen | though | thumb |

Silent *b*	Silent *t*	Silent *gh*	*gh* = /f/

6 **Complete signs and adverts a–e with words from 5.**

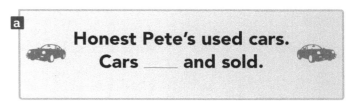

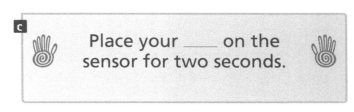

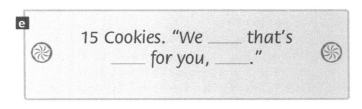

7 **Make it personal** Interview a classmate about their shopping habits e.g. *Where do you normally buy your clothes – online or in-store? Do you agree?*

5.3 Have you ever borrowed money from a relative?

1 Read the riddles a–e and complete the guesses.

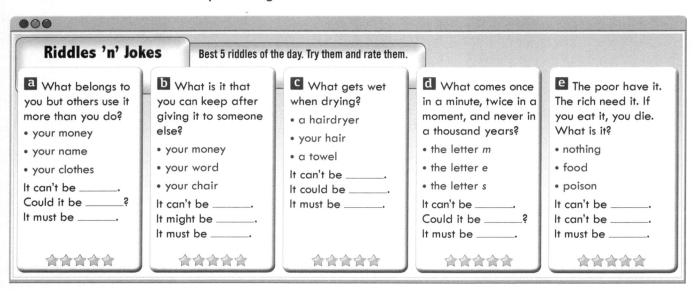

2 ▶5.6 Listen and match 1–3 to three of the signs a–e.

3 Match statements 1–6 to responses a–f.
1 There are figs on the menu.
2 I've just run 20 km.
3 Did you know that Lara doesn't drink milk?
4 The boss asked to speak with me in her office.
5 My credit card statement says I paid $60 for a pizza!
6 Have you seen that new movie? Absolutely terrible!

a Really? I guess she may be allergic or something.
b It could be a promotion. Good luck!
c That must mean that summer is nearly over.
d Come on! It got four stars. It can't be that bad.
e You must be exhausted. Come and sit down.
f What?! That can't be right.

4 Complete the mind maps with expressions from the box.

| be insane | be joking | be serious | be out of your mind | seriously expect me / us to believe that |

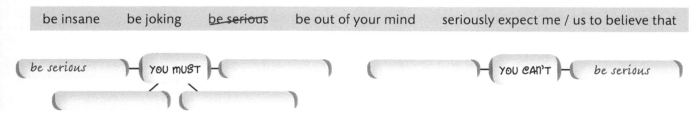

5 ▶5.7 Listen and check the phrases from 4 you hear. Pay special attention to the way final *t* and *d* almost disappear before consonants.

6 ▶5.8 *Express surprise.* Listen and express surprise with the prompts. Follow the model.
Model: *I just spent three thousand dollars on a designer bag. / be serious.*
You: *Three thousand dollars? You can't be serious!*

7 🅰 Make it personal Write down three names, places, or objects that are important to you. Then have a classmate speculate on why you have chosen them.

5.4 Have you ever bought a useless product?

1 Quickly read the article and match photos a–d to the four sale items.

Into bargain-hunting online? Here are a few examples of the most bizarre things ever sold on eBay's auction site:

— The owner of an F/A-18 Hornet fighter jet had bought it second-hand and had offered to have the plane restored for an incredibly low price of $9,000,000. After hearing of the **auction**, the FBI contacted the seller to **notify** him that he could only sell the plane to an American citizen residing in the United States. On top of that, the plane could not leave U.S. airspace; it was a matter of national **security**. Under these circumstances, nobody was prepared to participate in the auction.

— After Britney Spears had her hair cut off **completely**, the hair salon put it on eBay. The seller obviously saw the **opportunity** to make a small fortune. However, due to eBay's policy, the **ambitious** seller was not able to complete the **transaction**.

— One of the most interesting auctions happened in November 2005 when the original 1923 Hollywood sign was sold on eBay. The owner at the time wanted to sell it because he needed the money to finance a Hollywood project. A prospective buyer had a team of experts brought in to **certify** that it was indeed an original. **Luckily** it was, and the transaction was completed successfully.

— There are many **unbelievable** stories. A citizen of Australia tried to sell the country of New Zealand once. **Ridiculous**! There were a couple of bidders that day, but the auction suddenly stopped because it violated eBay's policy. I guess it's **impossible** to sell a country unless its people agree to it.

2 Reread. How many of the items were actually sold?

3 ▶ 5.9 Complete the suffix table with the 12 words in bold in **1**. Circle the stress. Listen to check.

Nouns	Verbs	Adjectives	Adverbs
a**b**ility	sol**u**tion	p**u**rify	g**o**rgeous	rem**a**rkable	d**e**sperately

4 Complete a–f with the correct form of the words in parentheses.
a Dial 1-800 334717 to _____ your reservation now. (**security**)
b I'd never used such a _____ product before. (**marvel**)
c The thing turned out to be a complete _____. (**disappoint**)
d The label said it was _____, but I guess I should've had it dry-cleaned. (**wash**)
e I love to see all those shirts _____ arranged on the shelves. (**nice**)
f The sales clerk said the cream would _____ my skin. (**pure**)

5 Are the adjectives in the statements in the correct order? Correct them if not.
a Last weekend I bought a beautiful, green dress at the mall.
b My grandfather is an old, kind man.
c I love my shampoo. It gives me shiny, gorgeous hair.
d I never really wear fashionable, new clothes.
e I live in a big, lovely house.

6 🔵 **Make it personal** Which of the statements in **5** are true for you? Change the ones that aren't.

7 📡 **Connect**
Try to find the weirdest item you can on eBay in five minutes. Send it to a classmate and ask them if they would buy it, and why / why not?

27

5.5 Do you often buy things on impulse?

1 Read the three headings in the article and choose the best title, a–c. Then read enough to confirm your choice.
   a How grocery stores get you to spend more.
   b How grocery stores get you to spend more – and what you can do.
   c The history of the grocery store.

It's all in the layout
Fruit and vegetables are usually the first thing you see when you enter the grocery store, but not the best thing to put at the bottom of your shopping cart. They do this so that you feel healthy after selecting them and then spend more on higher-priced, less healthy products. Have you ever gone to the store to buy some milk and come out with bags full of stuff? Essentials like bread and milk are usually hidden in corners, so that you pass by lots of other attractive produce when looking for them. With this in mind, get to know your grocery store's layout and plan where to visit first and last.

They attack your senses
Many grocery stores play slow, peaceful music as it makes you go round more slowly. Wear your headphones and listen to fast music when you shop. Grocery stores also use smells to attract you to certain areas. How often do you walk past the bakery section and think of delicious, fresh bread? Never go shopping when you're hungry. It won't affect you so much. Premium, expensive products are usually placed at eye-level, so make sure you look up and down when selecting what to buy.

Complicated pricing strategies
Grocery stores often use different measurements for products so that they look cheaper than they are. Always check the price per unit, in smaller text, on the shelf to compare prices. Also, that "3 for 2" offer may sound like a great deal, but remember that two products will always cost more than the one you went in there for.

2 Reread 1 carefully and circle the correct choice in a–f.
   a Fruit and vegetables are usually **near** / **far from** the entrance.
   b Bread and milk are usually **easy** / **difficult** to find.
   c Grocery stores want you to do your shopping **quickly** / **slowly**.
   d You should go shopping **before** / **after** you've eaten.
   e The **cheapest** / **most expensive** products are at the same height as your head.
   f You should check the **price** / **price per unit** to compare prices.

3 ⏵5.10 Order sentences a–f. Write customer (C) or sales clerk (SC). Listen to check.
   ☐ I just need to see your receipt, please.
   ☐ Can I exchange it for the 256 GB?
   ☐ I bought this flash drive yesterday and realized it's only 63 GB instead of the 256 GB I paid for.
   ☐ In that case I'm afraid there's nothing I can do.
   ☐ Seriously? But look, I have the bag.
   ☐ That's the thing. I threw it away, you see.

4 ⏵5.11 Complete the dialogue with five words from the box. Listen to check.

| card | cash | declined | exchange | insert |
| refund | stock | afraid | thanks | |

SA _____ or charge?
C Charge, please.
SA Thank you. _____ your _____, please.
C There you go.
SA I'm _____ it has been _____.
C I don't understand. Can you try this one?
SA It worked this time. There you are.
C Ah! At last!

5 ⏵5.12 *Dictation.* Listen and write down the dialogue. Check your answer in ⏵5.12 on page 58.

6 🔵 **Make it personal** When was the last time you returned something to a store? Discuss with a classmate.

Can you remember ...
▸ 6 technology words about shopping? SB→p. 58
▸ 3 things you can pay off? SB→p. 60
▸ ⊕ and ⊖ for the third conditional? SB→p. 61
▸ 5 modals of probability? SB→p. 62
▸ 2 examples of words with the suffixes -*ous*, -*ment*, and -*ness*? SB→p. 65
▸ adjective order? SB→p. 65
▸ three shopping problems SB→p. 67

6.1 What are you watching these days?

1 Read the article and put the words in the title in the correct order.

Makes / What / Addictive / Ever / Than / Today's / Before / Series / More / ?

☐ Sitting down in front of the TV to watch your favorite show is becoming a thing of the past. Binge watching, which means watching several episodes one after another, is growing, and it seems to be how more and more of us want our TV. The best show creators are beginning to understand that, too.

☐ According to him, the majority of 20th-century shows, including great dramas like *The Sopranos* and *Six Feet Under*, had episodes that worked independently. If you missed one, it didn't matter too much. In the early 2000s, shows like *24*, a series by Fox, started to change that. Viewers really needed to watch every episode to understand the story and soon, the 12- or 13-episode serialized drama had become a new American art form.

☐ The adult themes, antiheroes, and the art direction make them look like movies. But, while older shows focused on the characters, today's also focus on what happens next. Series creators are beginning to create stories that are less obvious. Series like *Stranger Things*, for example, tell stories with more unexpected occurrences and a lot more suspense.

☐ After watching our favorite series, we feel relaxed, our brains rest and our bodies fill with endorphins, our natural "feel-good substance". Maybe that's why we feel happy as soon as we turn the TV on and then watch several episodes at once to satisfy our "addiction".

☐ Before DVDs and Internet streaming, TV viewers had two choices: (1) watch whatever happened to be on, no matter how idiotic; or (2) turn the TV off and feel frustrated. Now we have a third: watch the shows we like, whenever we like, and for as long as we like. Serialized, streaming TV is perfect for keeping the endorphins flowing, and TV writers know it.

2 Circle the correct alternative in a–e and match the sentences to the paragraphs.
a TV producers **have** / **having** discovered this science, and by **use** / **using** new technology, they have given TV fans a third option.
b Apparently, **have** / **having** to watch more before you can understand what's going on makes modern series more and more addictive.
c How we watch TV **has** / **have** been changing in recent years.
d New series like *The Walking Dead* **is** / **are** similar to series from the past in some ways.
e D. B. Weiss, a writer for *Game of Thrones*, **told** / **said** *Newsweek* how he thinks things are changing.

3 Complete a–e with prepositions. Then reread the article. True (T) or False (F)?
a According _____ the article, some show creators have detected changes in traditional TV viewing patterns.
b Fox was very influential in changing TV shows at the end _____ the last century.
c Modern series usually have more complex storylines _____ series from the past.
d If you have to watch _____ a long time to understand a story, you get tired and stop watching.
e Today's viewers don't need to feel frustrated if there's nothing of interest _____ TV.

4 ▶6.1 Match both columns to form media words. Listen to check and mark the stress.
a sports   ☐ services
b medical   ☐ show
c reality   ☐ opera
d TV streaming ☐ events
e soap   ☐ media
f talk   ☐ show
g music   ☐ drama
h social   ☐ TV

5 ▶6.2 Listen to five dialogues and match items a–h in **4** to the speakers. There are two extra items.
1 The man's addicted to ☐.
2 This lady just loves ☐.
   The guy prefers ☐.
3 Both of them really like ☐.
4 They are both addicted to ☐.
5 They're always watching ☐.

6 🔘 **Make it personal** In pairs. What TV shows do you like to watch? How do you watch TV? When do you like to watch it? Share your favorite TV show with a classmate. Any similarities / differences?

I watch TV on my tablet after dinner.
I normally watch soap operas!

I love music shows, like The Voice. *I watch it on my phone while I'm on the bus.*

6.2 What's your favorite TV show ever?

1 Complete a–f with *a*, *an*, *the*, or prepositions. Read the article. True (T) or False (F)?

a ___ shows are ___ order ___ popularity.
b ___ U.S. has made more seasons ___ *Survivor* than the UK.
c ___ man ___ *The Bachelor* always proposes.
d People have become interested in baking again largely because ___ *The Great British Baking Show*.
e There is ___ range ___ different talents from contestants on *America's Got Talent*.
f All ___ ___ celebrities ___ *Dancing with the Stars* are extremely famous.

The Five Reality TV Shows that Had the Biggest Impact this Century

20 years ago, with the exception of the news and documentaries, the people on TV were all actors who had learned from scripts. There weren't many "real" people, but everything changed in 1997 with a show called *Survivor*. Now it seems reality TV is here to stay. Here are some of our favorites, in no particular order.

Survivor
Since starting in Sweden in 1997, dozens of different countries and regions have used the show's format. A cast of strangers are sent to an island or jungle location and have to live without modern luxuries until the final winner gets a prize. The British version only ran for two seasons, although there have been 37 seasons in the U.S.!

The Bachelor
This show focuses on a group of women who live together and compete for a handsome guy's marriage proposal. There have been four proposals in the British version since the show started in 2003.

The Great British Baking Show
Starting in 2010, this show invites a group of amateur bakers to compete against each other. Contestants aim to reach the final round by showing off their baking skills. The success of the show, both nationally and internationally, has been credited with renewing an interest in home baking, with some participants going on to become professional bakers.

America's Got Talent
Since its debut in 2006, this giant talent show created by Simon Cowell has attracted a huge number of weird and wonderful contestants to compete with a range of talents, including singing, dancing, magic, comedy, and more. Acts are judged by a panel of celebrities who change each season, and the winner receives a large cash prize.

Dancing with the Stars
Who wants to see a celebrity dance salsa? Apparently, millions of us do. This show became an instant hit in 2004. Part of the success comes from showing a vulnerable side of celebrities, some minor and some big names, as they struggle to learn a new skill.

2 Correct the mistakes in a–d and match them to the shows in 1.

a The contestant who she is leaving the island this week is Fifi.
b The women who lives in the house want to get married.
c The island what we chose is very beautiful.
d Sally baked a cake in the shape of Spider-Man, which it was inspired by the superhero.

3 Combine the two sentences in a–g with *that*, *who*, or *whose*.

a Nicki Minaj and Mariah Carey are judges. Their fights on camera were popular on Twitter.
b Catherine is the girl. She won the diamond engagement ring.
c The location is usually far away from civilization. The organizers choose it.
d Simon Cowell is a reality TV producer. His shows include *American Idol* and *The X Factor*.
e Kim's the woman. She won after the other 14 contestants left the island.
f He's chosen a song. The song is close to his heart.
g The dances can be difficult. The professionals teach them the dances.

4 ◉ 6.3 Cross out four relative pronouns that are not necessary. Listen to check and repeat.

HELP US IMPROVE YOUR TV
Please take a moment to complete our survey.

1 How often is the team that you cheer for on TV?
2 Are there any TV hosts that / who you can't stand? Who?
3 Would you like to see more shows that have "real" people?
4 Do you prefer movies that make you laugh or cry?
5 Are there any theme songs that you like to sing? Which one(s)?
6 Do you like news anchors who make jokes?
7 Are there any shows that you'd like to prohibit? Which one(s)?

5 Correct the mistakes with relative pronouns in three of the responses below. Then match the responses to the questions in 4.

a No, not really. I think it's a job where they should be serious.
b Every week. Botafogo, that are the best team in Brazil, play in the top league.
c Definitely. I hate all the actors are fake.
d I don't think shows have violence should be on in the daytime.
e Movies which make me laugh are more enjoyable than the ones that make me cry.
f Well, I like the one at the start of the news. Strange, I know!
g I hate the one who is on every Sunday. He's really annoying!

6 **Make it personal** Think of your own answers to the questions in 4. Share them with a classmate. Any surprises?

6.3 What was the last movie you saw?

1 Read and match 1–6 to a–g to make sentences. There is one extra.

1 The Marvel Cinematic Universe …
2 *The Avengers* has made …
3 *Star Wars* is popular …
4 The movies have made billions for …
5 *Harry Potter* is popular with …
6 The Harry Potter franchise …

a George Lucas over more than four decades.
b has made 20 movies in just 10 years.
c will probably have many more movies in the future.
d more money than any of their other movies.
e was filmed in the UK.
f all over the world.
g young and old movie fans.

2 ▶6.4 Read the online article and complete the bold phrases with *that*, *which*, *who*, or *whose*. Insert commas where necessary. Listen to check.

Hollywood franchises. A good one will make billions of dollars in ticket sales and brand-related merchandise for many decades.

MARVEL CINEMATIC UNIVERSE
19 MOVIES. $15 BILLION +

Marvel ____ **universe includes The Avengers, Iron Man, Captain America, Black Panther, and many more**, is the best-selling movie franchise of all time. This is topped by **The Avengers series ____ has made over 1.5 billion dollars**.

STAR WARS
8 MOVIES. $9 BILLION +

The franchise ____ has reached every corner of the planet. Eight movies, or 10 if you count *Clone Wars* and *Solo*, and more than four decades of comics, TV series, radio programs, toys, games, and other branded merchandise have been very profitable for **George Lucas ____ created and directed most of the movies**. May the force be with you, George.

J.K. ROWLING'S WIZARDING WORLD
$8 BILLION +

The magical franchise for both kids and adults was inspired by author J.K. Rowling ____ **novels sold millions of copies to all age groups**. The books ____ **were mainly written in a café**, have made her millions. It may take a few years, but it seems inevitable that there will one day be more battles involving the witches and wizards ____ **she created**.

3 Find the relative clauses in each description, and mark them restrictive (R) or non-restrictive (N).

Movies in three sentences!

Spider-Man, who was originally a Marvel superhero, has had six movies. The fourth one premiered in 2017 with a cast that included a new Spider-Man played by Tom Holland. Mary Jane Parker, who was the love interest between 2002 and 2007, was cut from the 2012 and 2014 movies.

Author Suzanne Collins, whose novels inspired four movies, must be pretty pleased with the amazing success of *The Hunger Games* saga. These exciting movies, which have captivated young adults worldwide, tell the story of a compulsory death match. It's a televised match that the contestants must win in order to survive.

4 ▶6.5 Insert two speech pauses (/) in four of sentences a–e. Listen to check and repeat with pauses and intonation. Which sentence doesn't have speech pauses? Why?
a *The Dark Knight* which is my favorite Batman movie won four Oscars.
b Heath Ledger who played the scariest Joker ever seen won an Academy Award after he died.
c Christian Bale who played Batman wasn't nominated for an Oscar for his part.
d Johnny Depp is the actor that has made Jack Sparrow so unforgettable.
e *Pirates of the Caribbean* which was inspired by Disneyworld's attraction has made over five billion dollars so far.

5 **Make it personal** What are your top three movies of all time? Why do you like them so much? Make a list then share it with a classmate.

31

6.4 Where do you usually watch movies?

1 **Complete the sentences with the words in the box in the correct form.**

| cast | clip | prequel | script | shoot | trilogy | view |

a Although it was released over 20 years later, *Star Wars: Episode 1* was actually a _____ to the earlier movies.
b Look! My new YouTube _____ has over a thousand _____ already!
c *The Lord of the Rings* is considered to be one of the most well-known _____ of all time.
d The new *X-Men* movie has an all-star _____.
e There are rumours that Steven Spielberg is going to _____ a new movie in Iceland, with a _____ he wrote himself.

2 ▶6.6 **Listen to this joke warning and answer a–g.**
a What's the name of the virus?
b Is it safe to touch?
c What can it destroy?
d What's the antidote?
e What are three places it can be found?
f Who should you send the message to?
g And if you can't do that, what does it mean?

3 ▶6.7 **Order words in a–e to make more advice for sufferers. Listen to check and repeat.**
a on / you / go / time / sure / make / home / .
b about / somewhere / a / think / vacation / taking / .
c enough / to / always / water / have / drink / .
d do / try / you / more / can / to / never / than / .
e take / more / you / efficient / you'll / if / breaks, / be / regular / .

4 **Rearrange the words in B's responses to make expressions of surprise.**
1 A: Did you know Angela has six dogs?
   B: kidding, / Really? / right? / You're
2 A: Phew! I've finally finished my homework!
   B: Thank / way! / goodness! No /
3 A: I've got 10 brothers and sisters.
   B: serious? / you / Are
4 A: My uncle's a movie director.
   B: out / here! / What? / of / Get

5 **Make it personal** Think of some surprising information about yourself or someone you know. Tell your partner. Was she / he surprised? Now tell another classmate. Who has the most surprising information? Whose reaction was the best?

My mom is an astronaut! She's been to the moon!

What? You're kidding, right?! Has she been to the moon?

Connect
Record yourself talking about the last movie you watched. Share it with a classmate. Have they seen it, too?

6.5 Who are the wildest celebrities you know?

1 Read the article. True (T) or False (F)?
   a All celebrities are famous for their talents.
   b If you don't look the same as others, people might think you're a celebrity.
   c After some time, you will become a dish such as soup or salad.
   d Your friends' sense of fashion is equally as important as your own.
   e If your father dresses like a chauffeur, everybody will think you are a star.

2 ▶ 6.8 Listen and choose the best summary.
   The girls are talking about:
   a what stars demand in their dressing rooms.
   b what female stars expect in their dressing rooms.

3 ▶ 6.8 Listen again and circle the correct answers in a–f. Check in ▶ 6.8 on page 59.
   a They say Beyoncé requires **baked** / **fried** chicken.
   b Katy Perry insists her room be **painted** / **furnished** in a **specific** / **colorful** way.
   c Lynn can't believe that Katy wants a **series** / **pair** of **French lamps** / **lights**.
   d Britney often requested a **picture of** / **photo that belonged to** Lady Diana.
   e Rihanna has a **long** / **short** list of things she likes to **eat** / **drink**.
   f If you get in free to **a Rihanna** / **an Adele** show, **you must** / **she will** give money to charity.

4 ▶ 6.9 Follow the model.

   I heard Adele wants chicken salad sandwiches in her dressing room. / No way!

   She wants chicken salad sandwiches? No way!

5 **Make it personal** Find a picture of a celebrity you like when they were younger. Share it with a friend and see if they can guess who it is.

Can you remember...
- 14 TV genres? SB→p. 72
- 2 ways of watching shows in other languages? SB→p. 73
- how to use restrictive relative clauses? SB→p. 75
- how to use non-restrictive relative clauses? SB→p. 76
- 5 expressions to show surprise? SB→p. 81

CHEAT'S GUIDE TO LIVING LIKE A STAR

We see them on TV and read about them in magazines. Today there is no escape from the celebrity lifestyle, and there is a growing number of celebrities who are famous for ... er, well ... being famous. But why go to the trouble of learning to sing, auditioning for a film, or embarrassing yourself on a reality TV show? Follow our tips and you could live the life of a celebrity, sort of.

1. **Get noticed.** This really is the most important part. If you look different and stand out from the crowd, people will want to know what your secret is (whatever you tell them, don't tell the truth!). Now, of course, we don't recommend that you instantly follow Katy Perry's example and be boiled in a pot with carrots before being presented as a meal. Start small and work up to becoming soup (or salad if that's what you prefer). Try a new hairstyle and maybe some accessories.

2. **Accessories.** Think of accessories as more than just clothes. Accessorizing is a lifestyle! From the phone you use to the friends you hang out with—everything has to make YOU look good. OK ... it might be that your current friends don't have the "right" sense of fashion and style to show you at your best. It's time to get serious. Drop those friends and find new ones that match your new glamorous lifestyle a little better. And if you can't find any new friends, get a dog.

3. **Followers.** Every celebrity needs followers. You know, those people who go around with them hoping to become famous as well. Of course, there are the professional followers, too—think security guards, drivers, photographers. You won't be able to afford all of these people just yet, but that shouldn't be a problem. Try asking your dad to wear a suit and sunglasses when he drives you to the mall; everybody will think he is your personal driver.

7   7.1 Does technology rule your life?

1 Read the article about designing your own app. What do you need to do when it's ready?

So you want to make your own app?

Want to make an app and sell it but have no idea where to begin? Well, first things first, ¹_____ down and don't worry! There are plenty of ways to ²_____ out what you need to know. You can ³_____ out a book from the library, read about it on the Internet, or you can even download an app to learn how to make apps! The list ⁴_____ on. Whatever method you choose, you'll soon find that you ⁵_____ up what you need to know quite easily.

But learning how to design your app and making it is just the first step. Once it's ready, you'll need a strategy to reach your clients. Essentially, you're ⁶_____ up a business. It's a very difficult market to ⁷_____ into as there are literally millions of apps out there. You'll need to be active in promoting it. So ⁸_____ down on relaxation time and get out there!

2 Complete the article in **1** with the verbs in the box in the correct form.

| break | calm | cut | find |
| go | pick | set | take |

3 ▶ 7.1 Match the words to make phrases related to technology. Listen and check and underline the stress.
  a distance   conferencing
  b movie streaming   app
  c video   time
  d screen   learning
  e online selling   theft
  f identity   platform

4 Which of the phrases in **3** can you see on the screens?

5 😀 **Make it personal** Have you ever had to call tech support or solve a tech problem? What was the problem? Did they / you resolve it? Tell a classmate.

34

7.2 What was the last little lie you told?

1 Read and complete the blog entry with *say* or *tell*.

Five little lies we tell our kids.

There are many lies we parents ¹_____ our children. We don't want to hurt or deceive them but to prevent potential problems from happening. Oh, and to make our lives easier, of course.
Here are five of the most common little lies.

1 "We're nearly there."
On any journey, of any length, whether it's a road trip or a short walk to the shops, we hear, every two minutes, "Are we nearly there yet?" The only possible answer to this is to ²_____, "Yes, nearly there." Never, ever ³_____ the truth. Even if you've still got three hours to go.

2 "Your picture is brilliant!"
In reality, the people have no bodies and the sky is underground, but we want them to feel good about it, so we ⁴_____ a little lie. If it really is good (for them), we'll ⁵_____ them so and stick it to the refrigerator.

3 "Sorry, there's no more ice cream left."
Well, at least until you go to bed. Then it's going to be an ice cream party down here! This is a good little lie to ⁶_____ for anything similar: candy, cake, cookies, whatever you want to eat. It's much easier to ⁷_____ this than to try and explain the importance of healthy eating. Especially when you're the one eating ice cream!

4 "We're leaving without you."
You're trying to leave the house, and they're taking forever to find their shoes, put them on, turn the TV off, etc. You ⁸_____ them you're in a hurry but it doesn't work. Finally, with no patience left, you ⁹_____ this and start to walk out the door. As if by magic, they're suddenly behind you fully dressed and ready to leave.

5 "We'll come back and buy it next time."
You know you definitely won't, but you ¹⁰_____ this because you know that they'll forget the next time you come. And you make sure you won't return for a long, long time.

2 Reread and answer a–e. Which lie 1–5 …

a is really a bit selfish because you want the same thing as your kids want?
b is one you tell when you hope they won't remember something?
c is one you should always tell when you're traveling somewhere?
d do you tell to scare them to do something more quickly?
e is one you tell to make them feel good?

3 ▶ 7.2 Diana's parents told her the five lies from **1**. Change the underlined pronouns and verbs in lies 1–5, and complete her complaints. Listen to check.

They lied to me!

1 They said _____
But it was another three hours!

2 They said _____
But the people looked like cows!

3 They said _____
But I heard them eating it after I'd gone to bed!

4 They said _____
But I knew they wouldn't!

5 They said _____
But we haven't been back there for six months!

4 ▶ 7.3 Listen and report lies a–f with the correct pronouns (P) and verbs (V).

a He said the check ₍ᵥ₎_____ in the mail.
b He said ₍ₚ₎_____ ₍ᵥ₎_____ pay next time.
c She said ₍ₚ₎_____ ₍ᵥ₎_____ still be good friends.
d He told Carol ₍ₚ₎_____ ₍ᵥ₎_____ great.
e She told Tina ₍ₚ₎_____ ₍ᵥ₎_____ him for his money.
f He said it ₍ᵥ₎_____ never happened to ₍ₚ₎_____ before.

5 Use *told* to report Anna and Mark's dialogue, if possible. If not, use *said*. Change pronouns and verbs as necessary. Follow the model.

Mark: I'll marry you, Anna!
Anna: I've never been interested in marriage.
Mark: I know you love me, Anna!
Anna: I can't marry you, Mark! I'm in love with someone else.

Mark told Anna he would marry her.

I once told a friend / my mother that …

6 🔊 **Make it personal** What's the worst lie someone told you? Tell a classmate.

7.3 How much of your day is screen time?

1 ▶ 7.4 Listen to Mr. Keller's call. Who's he getting help from?

   a A help desk agent.
   b A friend who's good with computers.
   c His wife of 20 years.

2 ▶ 7.4 Which five questions a–g did you hear? Listen again to check.
   a What kind of tablet do you have? ☐
   b Have you installed iTunes on your computer? ☐
   c What are you talking about? ☐
   d Are you familiar with the different icons? ☐
   e Do you have a Mac or a PC? ☐
   f When did you buy it? ☐
   g How can I upload music to my tablet? ☐

3 ▶ 7.5 These indirect question phrases are in phonetics. Can you decipher them? Listen to check and repeat.
   a /kən jʊ tel miː/
   b /aɪ wʌndə(r) ɪf/
   c /aɪ hæv noʊ aɪdɪə ɪf/
   d /aɪ niːd tə noʊ ɪf/
   e /də jʊ noʊ ɪf/
   f /də jʊ hæv eniː aɪdɪə/
   g /kəd jʊ tel miː/

4 Change a–g in 2 to indirect questions. Use the phrases from 3.
   a *Can you tell me what kind of tablet you have?*
   b *I wonder if* _____.
   c _____
   d _____
   e _____
   f _____
   g _____

5 ▶ 7.6 Listen to the random question generator and change the questions into indirect questions.

RANDOM QUESTION GENERATOR
THEY WANT TO KNOW . . .
A *how old I am.*
B _____
C _____
D _____
E _____
F _____

6 ▶ 7.7 Write the words with **bold** letters in the correct sound column. Listen and repeat a–e to check.
   a Never p**u**ll the pl**u**g out by the power cable.
   b Please p**u**sh the green b**u**tton to c**u**t off the power.
   c P**u**t this c**u**shion **u**nder you to get more c**o**mfortable.
   d If you can't sh**u**t the browser window, it might be a b**u**g.
   e Don't let your noteb**oo**k inbox get too f**u**ll.

ʊ   ʌ

_____   _____
_____   _____
_____   _____
_____   _____
_____   _____
_____   _____
_____   _____

7 **Make it personal** Share your answers to 5 with a classmate.

7.4 Are machines with personality a good idea?

1 **Thais is telling her sister about the questions in her oral test yesterday. Read what she said and complete the original questions.**
   a First they asked how old I was. "How old _are you_?"
   b They asked what I did last weekend. "_____ last weekend?"
   c They asked if I liked studying. "_____ studying?"
   d They asked when I would finish school. "When _____ school?"
   e They asked if I was going to have a party. "_____ going to have a party?"
   f They asked how much my English had improved. "How much _____ English _____?"

2 **Correct the mistakes in sentences a–e.**
   a Sue asked me to not call her tonight.
   b I asked her where was she going.
   c She asked me why did I want to know.
   d I told her to not be rude to me.
   e She said me to leave her alone.

3 **A traveler is going through customs with a new phone. Are a–h requests (R) or real questions (Q)?**
   a Did you buy that phone in this country, madam?
   b Can you let me see it, please?
   c Do I have to pay duty on it?
   d How am I supposed to do that?
   e Could you hold on while I ask my supervisor?
   f Which carrier are you using?
   g Can you get a signal here?
   h Would you fill out this form, please?

4 ▶7.8 **Match a–g to the gaps in the blog. Listen to Andy talking to a friend to check.**

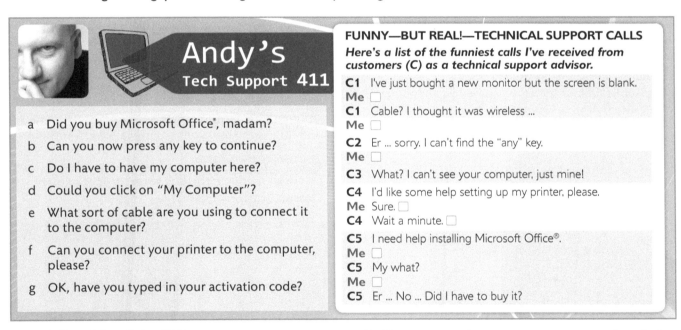

Andy's Tech Support 411

a Did you buy Microsoft Office®, madam?
b Can you now press any key to continue?
c Do I have to have my computer here?
d Could you click on "My Computer"?
e What sort of cable are you using to connect it to the computer?
f Can you connect your printer to the computer, please?
g OK, have you typed in your activation code?

FUNNY—BUT REAL!—TECHNICAL SUPPORT CALLS
Here's a list of the funniest calls I've received from customers (C) as a technical support advisor.

C1 I've just bought a new monitor but the screen is blank.
Me ☐
C1 Cable? I thought it was wireless …
Me ☐
C2 Er … sorry. I can't find the "any" key.
Me ☐
C3 What? I can't see your computer, just mine!
C4 I'd like some help setting up my printer, please.
Me Sure. ☐
C4 Wait a minute. ☐
C5 I need help installing Microsoft Office®.
Me ☐
C5 My what?
Me ☐
C5 Er … No … Did I have to buy it?

5 **Reread. True (T) or False (F)?**
   a C1 can't use his monitor because he has the wrong type of cable.
   b C2 thinks "any key" is a specific key on the keyboard.
   c C3 doesn't understand what "My Computer" is.
   d C4 can't set up his printer because he hasn't got his computer.
   e C5 can't install MS Office® because she has the wrong activation code.

6 ▶7.9 **Report the requests or commands to help an elderly lady at the doctor's. Tell her what the doctor said. Follow the model.**
   Doctor: Sit down.
   He asked you to sit down.

   Doctor: Could you please open your mouth?
   He asked you to open your mouth.

7 🎤 **Make it personal** What are your answers to 1? Share with a classmate.

7.5 How often do you use a pen?

1 Match a–f to 1–6 to make activities.

a social	1 reading
b visiting	2 online movies
c studying for	3 video games
d leisure	4 museums
e playing	5 networking
f watching	6 class

2 🅜 **Make it personal** Make a–d true using activities from **1**.

a I consider _____ much more interesting than _____.
b _____ is one of the most boring activities ever!
c I spend more time _____ than _____.
d I really should spend less time _____.

3 Match three of a–f to the student's notes, then abbreviate the other three.

a "The author states that the Internet is actually responsible for keeping people apart."
b "These days, more people send texts than call."
c "Fathers and mothers seem to find less time to spend with their children."
d "Libraries have fewer customers now."
e "The book said four out of ten students cannot read when they finish primary school."
f "Playing games is the most common use of smart phones for the under-15 age group."

Notes

○ 40% sts can't read when finish prim. sch.

○ net keeps ppl apart

○ parents spend less time w/ children

4 Rearrange the words to complete the conversations.

1 A: *that / We / deny / can't* robots will do all our jobs in the future.
   B: *disagree / I / totally.* There are some jobs only humans can do.
2 A: That guy on the TV is speaking nonsense.
   B: Well, *agree / disagree / may / you / or,* but *points / he / valid / some / makes.*
3 A: No, they don't think …
   B: *second. / finish / a / on / me / let / Hold.*
4 A: Translation technology nowadays is excellent.
   B: Yeah, *more / couldn't / I / agree.*
5 A: I think teens spend too much time on the Internet.
   B: *true / be / That / may,* but *think / you / don't* there are some benefits to it?
6 A: Well, *mean / depends / it / what / by / on / you* "advantages", exactly.
   B: *exactly / point / My!*

5 Order the words to make "discussion" phrases. There's one extra word in each.

a by / of / what / depends / you / on / mean / it / …
b let / hold / on / finish / me / in / a / second / .
c that / can't / deny / to / we / …
d true, / that / be / is / may / but / …
e be / more / agree / I / couldn't / .
f totally / am / disagree / I / .

6 ▶ 7.10 Listen to six extracts from pp. 94–95 in the SB, and number expressions a–f in **5** as you hear them.

7 🅜 **Make it personal** How much time have you spent on social media in the last seven days? Compare with a classmate. Any surprises?

Can you remember …

▶ 8 phrasal verbs? SB → p. 87
▶ 5 verbs for using a computer? SB → p. 90
▶ 1 verb to report a command? SB → p. 93
▶ 1 verb to report a request? SB → p. 93
▶ 6 phrases for expressing your views? SB → p. 95

8.1 How important are looks?

1 ▶ 8.1 Listen to the podcast. Which photo shows Lily, and which shows Kate?

2 ▶ 8.1 Listen again. True (T) or False (F)?
a Lily doesn't like her natural looks.
b Whenever she takes a selfie, something goes wrong.
c Lily thinks it's fine to use filters and change photos before posting them.
d Kate posts selfies every day.
e She sometimes gets a friend to help her.
f She doesn't care if people don't like her selfies.

3 Complete the extracts from the podcast with photography words.
a No, you see I'm really camera- ..., I hate it when people take my photo.
b I never get the right angle, or it comes out with ...-eye.
c Or even worse, I get ... by a bird or something!
d I love all the apps you can get to ... selfies.
e Nobody can tell they've been ...!
f Then I use a couple of different apps to ... the image.

4 Read the article quickly and choose the correct summary.
a The writer thinks fake videos are a good thing.
b The author thinks fake videos are a bad thing.
c The author thinks there are both good and bad things about fake videos.

Can we trust what we see?

It's common knowledge that most of the human images we see in magazines and on social media have been retouched or perfected, but the same is now fast becoming true for videos, with extraordinary consequences.

The idea of fake videos has been around for ages, from YouTube pranks to funny "bad lipreading" videos, but recently, researchers at the University of Washington shocked the world by producing an entirely false video of Barack Obama giving a speech. What they did was take different audio extracts from talks, interviews, and speeches he's given, then use AI to create a video of him giving those talks. The technology was originally designed to improve video conferencing, as the audio is usually good on calls, but the video, taking up more bandwidth, often stops or isn't very good quality. Researchers hoped video calls could keep the audio true, but use AI to create much higher quality videos.

At the moment, this technology can only be used for one person speaking, and they can only produce a headshot. But that is changing fast, with new developments using a source actor to create gestures and facial expressions to apply to a different face. The system is also beginning to work with multiple actors / speakers. This could have useful consequences for videodubbing of foreign movies, making it much more realistic.

But this rapidly developing system brings negative consequences, too. "Fake news", a real problem around the world, especially in politics, could become an even bigger worry, as people are able to create entirely fake videos of national leaders and other important politicians. Whilst solutions are being developed to try to prevent this, nobody knows what lies ahead for video technology.

5 Reread. True (T) or False (F)?
a Fake videos are a new thing.
b Researchers created a fake video from real audio.
c They wanted to improve video conferencing.
d At the moment the fake videos show a person's whole body.
e Fake videos could cause problems in the future.

6 🗣 **Make it personal** Do you think fake video technology is a good or bad thing? Why? Discuss with a classmate.

8.2 Do you like watching illusions?

1 **Match statements 1–5 to the responses.**

1 What was that loud bang? Was it a gun?
2 Hank and Sue are late again.
3 Kate still hasn't finished that report.
4 Enzo didn't pass the exam.
5 I arrived at the office at 4:30 p.m., but there was nobody there.

a Oh, she will. She can't have forgotten.
b They must have gone home early.
c They must have got lost again. They never take their GPS.
d No. It might have been a car or motorbike engine.
e Well, he can't have studied very hard.

2 ▶8.2 **Complete a–e with *must have*, *might have*, or *can't have* + the verbs below. Listen to check.**

| be | come | oversleep | see | win |

a The thief _____ in through that window. Look—it's still open.
b **A:** A woman answered the phone. I guess it was his wife.
  B: It _____ his wife. She died last year.
c The players look so happy. They _____ the match.
d Janet is late today. She _____.
e You _____ my sister last week. She was working in China.

3 **Look at the photo of a "floating man." How do you think he does this illusion?**

4 ▶8.3 **Listen to Josh and Alicia discussing the "floating man". Do they mention any of your ideas?**

5 ▶8.3 **Complete the extracts with the modal perfect and the verbs in parentheses. Then listen again and check.**

a He _____ (**be**) actually floating!
b He _____ (**have**) wires connected to his back.
c I think he _____ (**have**) a special frame under his body.
d It _____ (**be**) a very strong frame.
e ... which he _____ (**hide**) under that rug on the ground.

6 ▶8.4 **Listen and rephrase with *must've*, *might've*, or *can't 've*. Follow the model.**

> Maybe he ate something bad.

> He might've eaten something bad.

7 🟢 **Make it personal** What's the best street performance you've ever seen? Tell a classmate.

8.3 Have you ever cut your own hair?

1 Read Sam's email and order these items as she mentions them, 1–3. Match each one to her feeling about it.

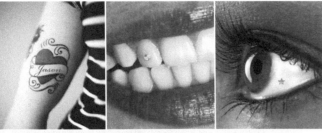

☐ too expensive   ☐ not available where she lives   ☐ did it but regrets it

Hi Ada,
Hope everything's OK with you.
Listen, I need your help! Can you call me when you get this, please? Only you can understand what I'm going through now. You know Jason and I have been planning our wedding for ever. Ever since we got engaged last month I've been thinking about what to do to mark the date. Remember that eyeball jewel implant we saw in Amsterdam? I decided to have that, but I found out you can't get it done here. Can you believe it? Anyway, Jason gave me this gorgeous ring, so I decided to have a little diamond put in my front tooth to match it. But, wow, when I talked to the dentist, I realized I couldn't afford that, no way.
Well, to cut a long story short, last week I decided to get a tattoo on my arm—it's a red heart, with "Jason" in the center. I was surprised it didn't hurt more to be honest. But then, you'll never guess what happened on Saturday. Jason broke up with me. Really. Just like that! I think he's found somebody else, but he says he hasn't. We'll see. Anyway, now I just have to lose this tattoo. You're having yours removed with a laser, right? Should I do it now or wait a while? Please call me a.s.a.p.
xoxo,
Sam

2 ▶ 8.5 Write four sentences to summarize the information in the email in **1**. Listen and compare.

She wanted to speak to Ada but sent her an email instead.
a She wanted to get a jewel …
b She thought of getting …
c She got …
d Now she …

3 Reread. True (T), False (F), or don't know (D)?
a Ada must be Sam's best friend.
b Sam and Jason had been engaged for a long time.
c Sam threw away Jason's ring.
d The tattoo took ages to do.
e Sam was expecting to split up with Jason.
f Jason might have a new girlfriend.
g Ada and Sam both have tattoos and want to laser them off.

4 ▶ 8.6 Listen and rephrase the sentences. Follow the model.

Model: *I have my hair cut at the hair salon. Yesterday.*
You: *I had my hair cut at the hair salon yesterday.*

5 Answer the questions in the ⌁D Task Manager to find what you should do with tasks a–g, and add three more of your own.
a clean / room
b cut / hair
c clean / something (what?)
d redecorate / something (what?)
e make dinner
f manage your social network
g fix / something (what?)

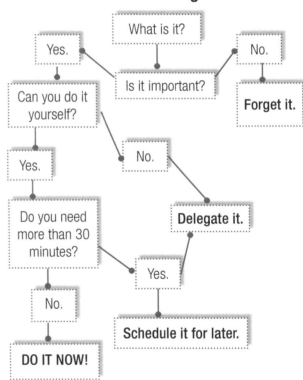

⌁D Task Manager

6 🎧 **Make it personal** For each item in **5** you delegate, make a statement like this:

I'm going to get my (teeth cleaned). I'll ask (my dentist) to do it.

7 📶 **Connect**

Go to draw.io and make a flowchart to help you make a decision about something. Send it to a friend and ask them if it helped them make a decision

8.4 Do you have a lot of furniture in your room?

1 Use the clues to complete the crossword.

Across
1 Put a glass of water on me and your alarm clock.
3 Put your books in me.
5 Sit on me.
7 Look at me and see yourself.
8 Rest your head on me.
10 Sleep on me.

Down
2 Fold and put your clothes in me.
4 Sleep under me.
5 Hang your clothes in me.
6 Switch me on to see.
9 Put me on the floor.

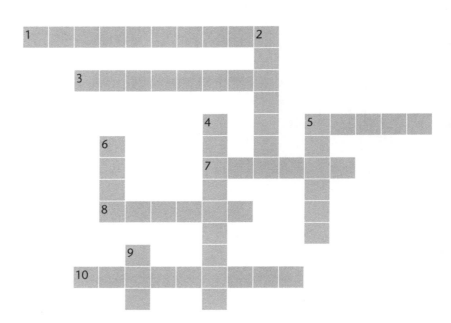

2 Read the first paragraph of the article, and circle the correct alternative in a–c.
a More / Fewer people are living in cities.
b Apartments in a few / many cities are getting smaller.
c Designers are / aren't adapting to the changes.

The world is urbanizing, and, with more and more people living in a small space, we are seeing changes in the houses and apartments we live in. One of the biggest, or should I say smallest, changes is in the size of our living space. Modern apartments, from New York to Tokyo and London to Rio, are getting increasingly smaller, and therefore, we are having to find interesting new ways to make everything fit. Here is our favorite space-saving design of the week.

The BedUp
At night it looks like any other ¹_____, but when you wake up in the morning you can lift the ²_____ up so that it is suspended from the ³_____. Imagine the space you can save—3 square meters to be exact. Under the ⁴_____ is a ⁵_____ so that you can work during the day. Small ⁶_____ in the bottom of the ⁷_____ give plenty of light so you can see what you are doing. At night you clear the top of your ⁸_____ and the ⁹_____ drops back to the ¹⁰_____, ready for you to climb in and go to sleep. Genius!

Come back next week for more top designs!

3 Read the second paragraph and complete 1–10 with these words. You can use each word more than once.

| bed | ceiling | desk | floor | lamps |

4 ▶ 8.7 Complete a–g with tag questions. Listen to check and repeat. Pay attention to the intonation and mark the tags ↗ or ↘.

Random Question Generator
a You're not American, _____?
b It's hot today, _____?
c You like soccer, _____?
d You had an English class yesterday, _____?
e The teacher won't give a test this week, _____?
f You'll finish your homework soon, _____?
g You'd like a coffee now, _____?

5 🎤 **Make it personal** Record a description of your house or apartment for a partner, then share it with them. Use all the words in the puzzle in **1**.

8.5 What's the hardest part of language learning?

1 Read the article and match the headings to paragraphs a–d. There are two extra.

- Mix your methods
- Read a lot
- Don't be afraid!
- Open your ears
- More than the language
- Guessing is good

Four language learning hints

Learning a new foreign language is hard work—but there are things you can do to make it quicker and easier. Read on to find out.

a _____
We spend most of our "communication time" listening, so this is obviously an essential skill to develop. But how? Living abroad is expensive and language classes don't always focus on listening. Well luckily for you, sound is all around you—from songs to streamed TV shows to podcasts. All you need to do is find the time to put your headphones on. A little every day is best.

b _____
How you feel about the language is the key to progression. If you learn about the culture behind the language, you will understand more about the language itself and feel more comfortable speaking with fluent speakers.

c _____
Sometimes we don't know exactly what a word means, even in our own language, and that is fine. In a foreign language this obviously happens more often, so learn to relax about it. Now, dictionaries are great and every language student should have one, but don't pick it up for every word you don't know. Instead, learn to focus on the words you know and trust your guesses for the ones you don't.

d _____
This is the most important tip of all. It doesn't matter how many conjugations you know or how much vocabulary you've studied. If you are paralyzed with fear when you have to produce it, it is all a wasted effort. Everybody will be pleased that you are trying; the more you try, the better you'll feel, and the better you feel, the more you'll want to learn. So forget your insecurity. Hold your nose and jump in! Mistakes are learning opportunities. The more you speak, the quicker you will improve. So go for it!

2 Reread and underline:
  a three things to listen to.
  b a problem with studying in another country.
  c a way to feel better when talking to fluent speakers.
  d advice for looking up words.
  e two things that happen when you make an effort to speak.

3 ▶ 8.8 Add a suffix (*-ion*, *-ive*, *-ly*, *-ial*, *-able*, *-ity*) to form a word from the text, making the necessary changes. Mark the new stress and listen to check.
  a comfort_____
  b communicate_____
  c essence_____
  d expense_____
  e insecure_____
  f obvious_____

4 ▶ 8.9 Complete comments a–e with one word, and correct one mistake in each. Listen to check.

a I agree! Speaking is more important then reading and writing. But they are _____ important, too. *Posted by NYAL*

b I'm much _____ at reading than listening and I want improve. Thanks for the tips! ☺ *Posted by EdBoy*

c I watched two episodes of a TV show online, but I couldn't understanding _____ of them. ☹ *Posted by Cori*

d I love listening! But I prefer American accents _____ British ones. They are more easier to understand. *Posted by Kweli*

e @Kweli, do you think? I can't understand _____ of them. I more prefer non-native accents like Japanese or German. *Posted by GlobalGirl*

5 🎤 **Make it personal** Write a comment about your listening skills. Use the comments in 4 to help you. Share it with a friend. Do you agree?

Can you remember ...
- 7 phrasal verbs about photography? SB→p. 99
- the difference between *must have*, *might have*, and *can't have*? SB→p. 100
- how to use the causative with *have* and *get*? SB→p. 103
- 11 furniture words? SB→p. 104
- rules for tag questions in ⊕ and ⊖ statements? SB→p. 105
- how intonation changes the function of tag questions? SB→p. 105
- 3 ways to predict information when listening? SB→p. 106

43

9   9.1 Does crime worry you?

1 ▶9.1 Circle the word with the different underlined sound. Listen to check.

a	a br<u>i</u>be	the pol<u>i</u>ce	a sp<u>ee</u>ding fine
b	a cr<u>i</u>me	to k<u>i</u>dnap	v<u>i</u>olence
c	organ<u>i</u>zed	p<u>i</u>racy	to go to pr<u>i</u>son
d	a cred<u>i</u>t card	to st<u>ea</u>l	stat<u>i</u>stics

2 ▶9.2 Listen to extracts 1–4. How many times do you hear the sounds in the pictures?

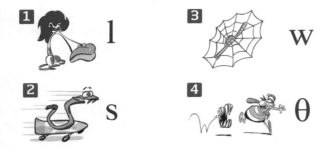

3 ▶9.2 Listen again and write the extracts.

4 Complete the table. Mark the stress on the words you write.

Crime	Criminal	Verb
br**i**bery		to _____ (sb)
b**u**rglary	a _____	to break into (a house)
drug dealing	a drug _____	to _____ drugs
_____	a kidnapper	to kidnap (sb)
m**u**rder	a _____	to murder / kill (sb)
r**o**bbery	a robber	to _____ (a person / a place)
theft	a _____	to steal (sth)

5 Change the underlined words to rewrite a–f.

a In the movie *Psycho*, Norman Bates <u>murders</u> travelers. In *Psycho*, the character Norman Bates is a _murderer_.
b A recent report says the number of <u>bribes</u> paid to politicians round the world tripled between 2015 and 2018.
  _____ in politics tripled over three years round the world according to a recent report.
c <u>Kidnappers</u> have taken a local businessman and are demanding money.
  Criminals _____ a businessman and are holding him until they receive cash.
d The Mafia is an international <u>criminal organization</u>.
  The Mafia is an international group that specializes in _____.
e Three men <u>robbed</u> the bank yesterday and got away with over $5,000.
  There was a _____ at the bank yesterday.
f The police are looking for a female suspect after the <u>theft</u> of a painting from a museum.
  The police are searching for a woman after she _____ a painting from a museum.

6 ▶9.3 Listen to a tour guide and answer a–d.

a Who is the man in the photo?
b Where did he live?
c Who was Herbert Hoover?
d Why did the man in the photo finally go to prison?

7 ▶9.4 Complete extracts a–d with the verbs in parentheses in the simple, continuous, perfect, or perfect continuous tense. Listen to check.

a You _____ at the site of one of the most famous Chicago legends. (**look**)
b _____ you _____ who lived at the Lexington Hotel? (**know**)
c Oh yeah! I _____ about him. (**hear**)
d They arrested him because he _____ tax for many years on his illegal money. (**not pay**)

8 🅰 Make it personal What famous crimes have there been in your country? Discuss with a partner.

9.2 How could your city be improved?

1 ▶9.5 Put the words in a–d in order to make sentences. Cross out one extra word in each. Listen to check.

   a   named / of / innovative / the / was / most / Medellín / world's / recently / city / .
   b   was / different / were / eight / judged / by / it / criteria / .
   c   and / created / communities / was / public / government / reached / spaces / were / programs / these / .
   d   neighborhood / by / a / considered / dangerous / once / this / was / slum / .

2 Read the web comments and mark them ⊕ positive or ⊖ negative.

What makes you proud of your city?

Isabel: My favorite singer, Shakira, ¹_____ born here. *9 months ago*

Jed: Help! I ²_____ surrounded by idiots all the time. I need to get out of here! *11 months ago*

Caitlin: Well, I just love the Statue of Liberty. It ³_____ given by the French. *11 months ago*

Jose: We have a beautiful park that ⁴_____ filled with trees and birds. It's very peaceful. *1 year ago*

Donna: Er, let's see. There ⁵_____ the place … oh no, wait. How about all the … hang on. We have a great … nope, nothing. *1 year ago*

Simon: We have the world's first subway system. It started in 1863—but it ⁶_____ updated a lot since then! *18 months ago*

3 Complete the comments in **2** with the verb **be**. Which one is not the passive voice?

4 Read the article and match the headings 1–4 to paragraphs a–c. There's one extra heading.

   1 Global success ☐
   2 Birth of a system ☐
   3 Quality not quantity ☐
   4 How it works ☐

URBAN MOBILITY

BRT system in Curitiba

a   When the city of Curitiba, Brazil, hit one million inhabitants in the 1970s, it couldn't afford a $300-million subway system. So <u>somebody developed an alternative system</u>, the Bus Rapid Transit (BRT). Today, <u>people consider it</u> a success because it combines the speed of trains with the low cost of buses.

b   <u>People often compare Curitiba's bus system</u> to a subway system: exclusive lanes, pre-paid ticket counters, good quality stations, and sensors that communicate with smart traffic lights. Today, <u>Curitiba's 2.3 million residents use its buses</u> to commute to work quickly and efficiently.

c   <u>People have adopted the BRT system</u> in 83 cities worldwide, including Guangzhou, one of China's fastest-growing cities, and <u>the Canadian government will soon implement it</u> in parts of Saskatoon.

5 Transform the underlined phrases in **4** to the passive voice. Only use **by** + **agent** if necessary.

6 ▶9.6 Transform what you hear into the passive voice. Follow the model.

   We have made a lot of progress.

   A lot of progress has been made.

7 🔵 **Make it personal** What makes you proud of your city? Think of the top three things, then share with a classmate. Any surprises?

45

9.3 Have you ever been to court?

1 ▶9.7 Listen to two friends discussing a news story. Check the correct headline.

> 19-year-old arrested for illegal downloads: 13 GB found on hard drive
> NY teen arrested for selling movie before official release date

2 ▶9.7 Listen again. True (T) or False (F)?
- a All of Peter's downloads were illegal.
- b He was sentenced to five years in prison.
- c He shared a download link for *Toy Story 4* on the Internet.
- d He made a lot of money selling the movie.

3 ▶9.8 Listen to the rest of the dialogue. Are these the opinions of the man (M), woman (W), or neither (N)?
He should:
- ☐ be acquitted
- ☐ do community service
- ☐ pay a fine
- ☐ be sentenced to life
- ☐ be sentenced to one year in prison

4 Match the start of criminal biographies 1–2 to two of endings a–c.

1. Adam Worth (1844-1902) was the original master criminal. At 17, he joined the American Union Army but was soon registered as "killed in action", giving him the opportunity to begin his criminal career. In 1869, when detectives were tracking him after a bank robbery in Boston, he decided to move to Europe. From there, he organized crimes such as illegal gambling in Paris, diamond thefts in South Africa, art thefts in England, and bank robberies in Belgium.

2. Today he is known as Frank W. Abagnale, but this is just one of nine identities he has used. Frank started by writing false paychecks for his various bank accounts. Then at 16, he decided to travel the world so he created an employee ID and pilot's licence and then phoned Pan Am airways claiming to be a pilot who had lost his uniform. With the right clothes, he flew around the world staying in five-star hotels and using fake checks, a life that inspired the movie *Catch Me If You Can*.

...

a. French police eventually caught him, but 12 other countries also wanted to charge him with fraud. After a year in prison in France, he spent six months in a Swedish jail. Next he was returned to the U.S., where he was sentenced to 12 years. After just five, the FBI approached him to work as a security consultant, a job that he still has today.

b. He moved first to Australia and then to Brazil. Four years later, the police discovered where he was hiding, but by that time he'd had a son and could not be extradited. He stayed in Brazil for 31 years before returning voluntarily to the UK to face the rest of his 30-year sentence. He spent eight years in prison, but was released just before his 80th birthday.

c. He earned the nickname "the Napoleon of Crime" for his various criminal activities and was also the inspiration for the character Moriarty: Sherlock Holmes' criminal adversary. He was eventually caught for a robbery in Belgium and sentenced to seven years in prison, although he was released after four for good behavior.

5 Reread and answer whether a–f are true of Adam Worth (A), Frank W. Abagnale (F), or both (B).
- a started committing crimes at a young age.
- b is no longer alive
- c was an international criminal
- d was released early
- e used his criminal experience legally
- f had a movie made about his life

6 ▶9.9 Listen and repeat the underlined extracts from 4. Notice the connections, schwas, and silent letters.

7 🎤 **Make it personal** Circle the correct preposition in a–e. Note your answers then share them with a classmate.
- a How much stress are you **under** / **with** at the moment?
- b Do you stop for a coffee **in** / **on** your way to work or school?
- c What is **in** / **on** the street corner near your house?
- d Have you ever waited more than an hour **for** / **to** a bus?
- e How many **from** / **of** your friends are the same age as you?

9.4 Where will you be living ten years from now?

1 ▶9.10 Listen and number the phrases, 1–10, as you hear them.

- [2] Want to go?
- [ ] Do you think he'll have stopped smoking?
- [ ] We'll be working tomorrow.
- [ ] We love beans cooked by your mother.
- [ ] It will spread across the park.
- [1] One, two, go!
- [ ] Do you think he loved hot smoking?
- [ ] It will be working tomorrow.
- [ ] It will have been cooked by your mother.
- [ ] Wheels, spread across the park.

2 Read the article and cross out the three unnecessary sentences.

Stay safe online

The boom in technology means that laptops, smart phones, and tablets are everywhere. Unfortunately, so are the criminals who are trying to get inside them. Read our security tips to learn how to protect yourself from cybercrime.

Tip 1: Make sure your anti-virus software is **up-to-date**. Let it expire before you renew it. Hackers are creating new viruses all the time and only the very latest software can truly protect you.

Tip 2: Get a **tracking** app. Tablets and smart phones are the perfect **target** for thieves. Download a tracking app so the police can follow your device and find it.

Tip 3: Use strong **passwords**. Combinations of numbers and letters are a good idea. Add capital letters, too, if you can. Try using your name and birthday—nobody will guess that! And don't use the same password for multiple accounts.

Tip 4: Click carefully. Don't **click** on links in emails and social networks, especially if you don't know where they came from.

Tip 5: Turn Wi-Fi off. If you can use your device as a Wi-Fi **hotspot**, protect it with a password and turn off the hotspot when you're not using it. Don't use the Internet at home. This will prevent other people signing in to your network.

3 Match the **bold** words in **2** to their definitions and examples a–f.

a _____ noun (C) an area with a lot of activity. A popular area. Usually two words but one when referring to the Internet. E.g. *This area was a crime _____ a few years ago, but it's safe now.*

b _____ verb (-ing, -ed) to follow evidence. E.g. *The hunters _____ the tiger through the forest.*

c _____ adj. very modern. E.g. *The surgeons used _____ techniques.*

d _____ noun (C) a thing you want to get, attack, or achieve. E.g. *Our sales _____ is 500 units per month.*

e _____ noun (C) a word or phrase that lets you enter. E.g. *You can't come in until you give me the _____.*

f _____ verb (-ing, -ed) select something on a computer screen by pressing a button. E.g. *Use the mouse to _____ on the icon.*

4 Rewrite a–e using **by**.

a You can make your computer more secure if you use virus protection software.
b The last guests arrived just before 10:00 p.m.
c Some hackers uploaded the malware.
d Midnight is the latest I'll be home. I may get home before that.
e Tony improved a lot because he worked hard.

5 ▶9.11 Listen to two colleagues. True (T) or False (F)? Is Sam A or B in the photo?

a Both men are looking forward to the weekend.
b Sam has to give his boss the report first thing on Monday.
c Sam is going to watch sport at the weekend.
d Sam likes the Lakers.

6 ▶9.11 Complete extracts a–d with three words in each. Listen again to check, and repeat.

a I think I _____ all the way through.
b He just gave it to me and he _____ Monday.
c Hopefully _____ finished in time to watch the game.
d If the Lakers win, my prayers _____ answered.

7 Write ⊕ or ⊖ future sentences in 1–3 about Sam and Phil. Use the verbs given.

1 Sam _____ (**have fun**) this weekend.
2 Sam _____ (**finish the report**) Saturday evening.
3 Phil _____ (**see his children**) this weekend.

8 🔵 **Make it personal** What do you do to stay safe on social media? Discuss with a classmate.

9.5 Do you watch TV crime dramas?

1 Read the headline and choose the best definition for the crime.

Man Charged with Arson After Cigars Catch Fire

a arson: *noun*. Smoking in public places.
b arson: *verb*. To play with fire.
c arson: *noun*. Burning something deliberately.

2 ▶9.12 Read and order the rest of the story, 1–5. Listen to check.

○ The insurance company refuses to pay the lawyer and he takes them to court. The judge decides that because the insurance company hadn't specified what kind of fire was unacceptable, they would have to pay.

○ So, have you heard the story about the lawyer and the cigars? Here's how it goes.

○ About a month later he contacts the insurance company to ask for his money because his cigars have disappeared in "a series of very small fires".

○ The insurance company pays the lawyer but then … they have him arrested for arson, saying that he had deliberately burned his own property to claim the insurance money!

○ A lawyer buys a box of very rare, expensive cigars. To protect them, he takes out an insurance policy so that if they are damaged he can receive some money.

3 ▶9.13 Listen to three dialogues. Match three of excuses a–e you hear to photos 1–3.
a Just hear me out.
b It's not what it looks like!
c It's not what you're thinking.
d It's not what it seems.
e I can explain.

4 ▶9.13 Listen again. True (T) or False (F)?
a Brad's computer had a problem and crashed.
b Brad's sorry for upsetting Yvette.
c Terry accepts responsibility for the kitchen.
d Terry's mother believes him.
e Leony's ex-boyfriend has sent her a text.
f Leony's sorry that Mark is upset.

5 ▶9.14 Look back and match lesson titles 9.1–9.5 to answers a–f. Listen to check and write the follow-up question each time.
a ☐ Er … I don't know. I guess I'll still be living in this city somewhere.
b ☐ No, of course I haven't!
c ☐ It doesn't really worry me too much. I live in a safe neighborhood and I've never been a target.
d ☐ Not really, no. They're not my favorite sort of program.
e ☐ I guess it would be better if there was more public transportation at night.

6 **Make it personal** Discuss your answer to the question in lesson title 9.1 with a classmate. Any surprises?

Can you remember …
▶ 10 crimes? SB→p. 112
▶ 4 verb aspects? SB→p. 113
▶ how to form the passive voice? SB→p. 115
▶ 6 punishments for crimes? SB→p. 116
▶ 2 verb tenses to talk about the future? SB→p. 119
▶ 5 phrases for giving excuses? SB→p. 121

10.1 What drives you crazy?

1 Match a–e to 1–5 to make quotes about anger. Which one suggests anger is positive?

a "Anger is never without reason,
b "When angry, count to four;
c "People won't have time for you
d "Don't make me angry.
e "When people are sad, they don't do anything.

1 You wouldn't like me when I'm angry." David Banner
2 They just cry. But when they get angry, they **bring about** a change." Malcom X
3 but **seldom** with a good one." Benjamin Franklin
4 when very angry, swear." Mark Twain
5 if you are always angry or **complaining**." Stephen Hawking

2 Match the **bold** words in **1** to their definitions.

_____ adv. not very often, rarely.
_____ verb make something happen.
_____ verb being negative about things.

3 ▶10.1 Match dialogues 1–3 to what has angered each person. There are two extra.
☐ bad drivers   ☐ insincerity   ☐ school   ☐ weather   ☐ work

4 ▶10.1 Listen again. True (T) or False (F)?

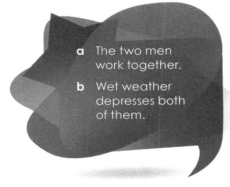

a The two men work together.
b Wet weather depresses both of them.
c The woman is driving.
d The man thinks she overreacted.
e The customer gave the cashier the exact money.
f The cashier annoyed both women.

5 ▶10.2 Listen and repeat a–e making the connections. Notice the silent letters.
a ups_and_downs
b little by little
c sick_and_tired_ of_it
d peace_and quiet
e again_and_again

6 ▶10.3 Listen to dialogues 1–5. At the beep, write the missing phrase, a–e, from **5**.

7 🗣 **Make it personal**   Share your favorite love, hate, or anger quote from **1** with a classmate.

49

10.2 What do you love to hate?

1 Read the article about pet hates and add these headings. There is one extra.

| Car modifications | Chewing gum |
| Eating on public transportation | Music in stores |

Things I Could Happily Live Without

By Karen Kaye

Getting irritated by the noise, dirt, or smell of an inconsiderate world? Here are the things I would prohibit to make life a whole lot more pleasant. Do you agree with me? Let's start a revolution!

1. _____
Extra loud speakers in the trunk so we can all hear your terrible music—inconsiderate. Neon lights under the vehicle—what's the point? And those terrible, noisy turbo engines—nobody needs to hear them. I would start my revolution by making these people take the bus!

2. _____
Have you ever seen a camel eating? This is what people look like when they put that horrible stuff in their mouths. And then, to make things even worse, nine times out of ten people stick it to seats, tables, bus windows, or just drop it on the ground. Ban the stuff, just like they did in Singapore.

3. _____
And another thing: I'm fed up with smelling other peoples' dinner when I'm stuck on a bus or on the subway. It makes me feel sick! Not to mention the paper and plastic that people leave. And then there's the risk of injury if they drop their hot coffee on me. Water might be OK, but only on hot days and make sure you take your bottle with you!

2 Reread the article and answer a–e.
   a Which problem does Karen feel is dangerous?
   b Which item is illegal in another country?
   c Which problem does not cause litter?
   d Which problem does Karen suggest a punishment for?
   e Which problem causes Karen to have a physical reaction?

3 ▶10.4 Complete the comments on the article with these verbs. Add a preposition if necessary. Listen to check and notice the /ŋ/ sounds.

| complain | listen | make | meet | stop | throw |

a Len 1 hour ago
If people showed a little more consideration, this city would be much nicer. We're all responsible _____ things better. Let's get out there and do it. No more gum! Viva the revolution!

b Lady1 2 days ago
Don't you think there are bigger things to worry about? Poverty, crime, violence. _____ these problems should be the priority.

c Crazyboy 2 days ago
Why don't you just stay at home and avoid _____ other people? Problem solved.

d SamSame 3 days ago
Not _____ your trash in the trash can is just laziness, there's no other excuse for it. It makes the city look really bad.

e Kimbo7 3 days ago
Hey! I enjoy _____ to my music when I'm driving. It's better than hearing people like you complain all the time.

f Fifi88 3 days ago
Instead _____ about people on the Internet, why don't you learn to be a little more tolerant?

4 Do the posts agree (A) or disagree (D) with the writer?

5 ▶10.5 Listen to five more comments. Write five words in each of a–e.

a @ Crazyboy
You _____. She's allowed to have her opinion.

b @ Lady1
Sure, nice idea. But who's _____? What can we do?

c @ SamSame
Honestly, I'm _____ that. When did a few pieces of paper hurt anybody?

d @ Kimbo7
Come on, you've got to admit it. She does _____.

e @ Len
_____ improving the city, sure, but banning chewing gum? Don't you think that's a little extreme?

6 **Make it personal** Add your own "pet hate" to the article in **1**. Share it with a classmate. Are they annoyed by the same thing?

50

10.3 How assertive are you?

1 Take our unit 10 preposition quiz. Complete the phrases in **bold** with a preposition.

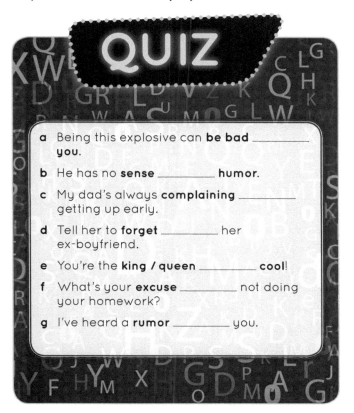

a Being this explosive can **be bad** _____ you.
b He has no **sense** _____ humor.
c My dad's always **complaining** _____ getting up early.
d Tell her to **forget** _____ her ex-boyfriend.
e You're the **king / queen** _____ cool!
f What's your **excuse** _____ not doing your homework?
g I've heard a **rumor** _____ you.

2 Complete sentences a–d with an infinitive and a gerund phrase using the given words.

a stop / ask for / directions
After driving for half an hour we realized we were lost, so we _____.
After we bought our new GPS we _____.

b try / open / the door
My hotel room was so hot because the a/c was broken. I _____ and windows, but it made no difference.
The other day I locked my keys inside the car! I _____ with a paperclip, like in the movies, but it didn't work.

c remember / visit / grandparents
I must _____ this weekend. It's their 50th wedding anniversary.
Do you _____ when you were a child? What did you do together?

d stop / buy / milk
After work I _____ because I had run out at breakfast.
My wife and I _____ after the health scares. They said on the news that it was dangerous.

3 *Tense review.* Complete the movie review with the best form of the verbs in parentheses.

Red, who _____ (**play**) by Jason Sudeikis, is a flightless bird who _____ (**live**) on an island with other flightless birds. Red has trouble controlling his temper, and one day he _____ (**order**) to take an anger management class, because he _____ (**break**) an egg when he _____ (**lose**) his temper. Soon the island _____ (**visit**) by a group of "friendly" pigs who are welcomed by the birds. Red becomes suspicious but nobody listens to him. One day, they wake up and find the pigs _____ (**destroy**) the island. Everyone is sorry they _____ (**not believe**) Red when he tried to warn them. Now the angry birds must attack Piggy Island to try and get their eggs back. Can they do it?

4 ▶10.6 Listen to five situations and respond after the beep using a–e with an infinitive or gerund.
a Why don't we stop (**have**) a break?
b I don't remember (**put**) them there.
c Have you tried (**drink**) some water?
d Could you please stop (**do**) that?
e Please, try (**remember**).

5 🎧 **Make it personal** What other movies do you know about an angry person? Share with a classmate.

6 📶 **Connect**
Go to brainyquote.com and find an interesting quote on hate or anger. Send it to a classmate and see what they think.

10.4 How similar are you to your friends?

1 Complete the brochure with *yourself*, *themselves*, or *myself*. Do you do any of these things?

Guide to Emotional Well-being

a ➡ Every day, repeat the phrase "I like _____, I like _____. I love _____!"

b ➡ See _____ as others see you. You'll be surprised how positive the impression is.

c ➡ Understand that if someone is treating you badly, they probably don't like _____ either.

d ➡ Do _____ a favor. Learn to be independent. Get out and do things on your own.

e ➡ Accept that everybody doubts _____ sometimes. It's natural, but you can learn to beat it.

2 Study these sentences. Match <u>phrasal verbs</u> 1–8 to definitions a–h.

1	Watching the news always <u>brings me down</u>.	a	tell somebody what to do
2	I never read the instructions for a new gadget, I just use it and try to <u>figure it out</u>.	b	become sick with something
		c	make somebody feel sad
3	My older sister used to <u>boss me around</u> all the time when we were young.	d	have an argument with somebody
		e	continue, not change your mind
4	I <u>get along well with</u> my parents.	f	have a good relationship with somebody
5	You look like you're <u>coming down with</u> a cold.	g	find the answer, understand
6	My wife always <u>lifts me up</u> when I'm feeling sad.	h	make somebody feel happier
7	I hate it when I <u>fall out with</u> my family.		
8	Once you've decided what to do, you should <u>stick to</u> it.		

3 ▶10.7 *Intuitive quiz!* Match 1–8 to the responses. Then complete with phrasal verbs from **2** and the correct object (or no object). Listen to check. How good were your guesses?

1 What's wrong? Are you sick?
2 I just don't know how to use this software.
3 Wow, you look great!
4 Oh, no, I failed my driving test!
5 Clara always tells me what to do.
6 I really wanted to stay in last night, but then John called and ...
7 Why aren't you speaking to Lisa?
8 Do you like your brother?

a Don't let it _____. You can always take it again.
b Oh, we _____ last weekend and had a fight.
c Ugh, I think I'm _____ the flu.
d Oh, yes, I _____ him.
e Let me see. I'm sure we can _____ together.
f You shouldn't let her _____ like that.
g Aw thanks! You always know how to _____.
h No, really? Don't let him change your mind! Decide what you want and _____!

4 ▶10.8 Listen again and say the correct response after the beep.

5 🎧 **Make it personal** Choose three of the questions or sentences in **3** and write your own responses. Read them to a classmate. Can they guess which questions or sentences they respond to?

52

10.5 What do you find hardest about English?

1 Match a–f to 1–6 to make quotes. Check your favorite.

a Learn from the mistakes of others. You …
b Don't be afraid of making mistakes. Be …
c Everyone makes mistakes. The wise are not …
d Anyone who has never made a …
e The greatest mistake you can make in …
f Nothing that is worth …

1 those who never make mistakes, but those who forgive themselves and learn from their mistakes. *Ajahn Brahm*
2 mistake has never tried anything new. *Albert Einstein*
3 can't live long enough to make them all yourself. *Eleanor Roosevelt*
4 learning can be taught. *Oscar Wilde*
5 afraid of not learning from them. *Anonymous*
6 life is to be continually fearing you will make one. *Elbert Hubbard*

2 ▶10.9 Proofread and correct students' sentences a–j. Four have no mistakes; the others have two mistakes each. Listen to a teacher giving the class feedback to check. How many did you get right?

a I told to her it is difficult and asked her to help me.
b A lot new hotels are building in my city.
c It started raining soon after we left the house.
d My dad complains to get up early in the morning.
e I can't remember where is the my car.
f Where did you get your eyes checked?
g Can you tell me who wrote this song?
h How long are you living this city?
i He was awarded an Oscar for his role in the movie.
j She works like a secretary for a company who specializes in import / export.

3 Circle the correct alternatives in the poster.

Our strengths and weaknesses in English

1 I **think / find** it easy **to read / read** in English but a little boring.
2 I'm not so good **to remember / at remembering** new words.
3 I have a lot of **difficulty / difficult** pronouncing "sh" and "ch."
4 **To listen / Listening** is very hard.
5 **It's / Is** difficult to speak without pausing a lot.

4 ▶10.10 Give the advice below to students 1–5 in **3**. Put the verbs in the correct form. Listen to five student-teacher dialogues to check.

a A good way of <u>improve</u> your pronunciation <u>be</u> <u>record</u> yourself.
b Try <u>focus</u> on the stressed words.
c How about <u>learn</u> some common phrases like "I mean" or "you know"?
d You should <u>consider</u> <u>read</u> things you <u>be</u> interested in.
e Have you <u>think</u> about <u>keep</u> a notebook for new words?

5 Look back through Student's Book units 6–10 and choose:

Page number:	Reason you chose this one?
The most interesting reading text.	
The best song line.	
The most difficult grammar point.	
The funniest cartoon in the Grammar section (p. 138–157).	
The most enjoyable listening / video.	

6 **Make it personal** Share your answers to **5** with a classmate. Do they agree?

Can you remember …

▸ 8 mood words? SB→p.124
▸ 6 binomial phrases? SB→p.125
▸ 4 verbs followed by a gerund? SB→p.126
▸ 4 words / phrases followed by *for*? SB→p.127
▸ 4 words / phrases followed by *of*? SB→p.127
▸ 3 verbs with a different meaning when followed by an infinitive or a gerund? SB→p.128
▸ 6 phrasal verbs? SB→p.132
▸ 4 phrases to describe strengths and weaknesses? SB→p.132
▸ 6 phrases for making recommendations? SB→p.133

Audio script

Unit 1

1.1
a What's something you just can't live without?
b What are you good at?
c What makes you nervous?
d Who are you closer to, your mom or your dad?
e What's the most fun place you've been to?

1.2
Romeo and Juliet is a famous play by William Shakespeare. Romeo Montague and Juliet Capulet are teenagers in Verona. They meet at a party and get along well immediately. Naturally, they fall in love, but, later, they discover that they belong to rival families. The Montagues and the Capulets are enemies. Their love is impossible, but also completely irresistible. This is the beginning of a tragic sequence of events. The lovers decide to escape with help from a friar. The friar marries them secretly, but they can't stay together. Romeo is exiled from Verona. The friar has a plan. He gives Juliet an herbal drink. She will "sleep" for 42 hours, enough for everyone to think she is dead. Then they will get together and leave Verona. Sadly, Romeo hears about Juliet's death, but doesn't know about the plan. He can't live without Juliet. He buys some poison, finds Juliet and kills himself. Juliet wakes up and, finding Romeo dead, she takes his dagger and kills herself, too. This classic romance has been an inspiration for generations of authors since.

1.3
B = Ben   M = Matthew

B I just couldn't finish reading *Antony and Cleopatra*. All those difficult words, bro.
M OK, here's the idiots' summary of the play. Caesar, Antony and Lepidus rule the Roman Empire.
B The three guys, right?
M So Antony is married to Flavia ...
B You mean Fulvia, right?
M Uh, yeah. Fulvia. So Antony is married to Fulvia, but they don't get along very well. She lives in Rome, he lives in Alexandria, Egypt, and cheats on his wife with Cleopatra, Queen of Egypt.
B Right! Antony and Cleopatra hang out together in Egypt. Woohoo ...
M Then Antony's wife, Fulvia, dies and he goes back to help Caesar fight the enemies of Rome.
B Then Antony and Caesar's sister get married. What's her name?
M Octavia. Right. But they soon drift apart and Antony goes back to Egypt and Cleopatra.
B I bet Caesar didn't like that!
M He didn't like it for sure. So Caesar and Antony fall out and start to fight for control of Egypt.
B What happened in the end?
M Antony heard false news of Cleopatra's death and killed himself. When Cleopatra heard the love of her life was dead, she committed suicide, too ...
B ... with small black poisonous snakes. Got it! Thanks a lot, man.

1.5
a Acquaintances generally aren't people you can count on.
b Friends are people you are usually in contact with.
c Good friends are people you hang out with and get along with. OR Good friends are people you get along with and hang out with.
d Very close friends are the people you can always rely on.

1.6
Here's something I've been giving a lot of thought to lately: friendship. Friendship is a sacred thing and I believe Facebook is cheapening it. I go on this Facebook, I see people with thousands of what they call friends, which is impossible. You can't have a thousand friends. Here's how you can tell who on Facebook is really your friend. Let's say on Friday, post a status update that says "I'm moving this weekend and I need help." The people that respond, those are your friends. Everyone else isn't. I would like people to start whittling this down. Here's an example of someone who has 545 friends: her name is Gina. Every five seconds, Gina has something to say—"100 degrees in San Diego, ugh," "Gina is eating other people's food," "Coffee," "Gina is watching *Weeds*," "Listen to Patti, people," "I should be watching *Oprah* right now," "Yay, my weekend just started," "Robin Thicke and mashed potatoes. Hollah!", "Can the time please change already?", "Who am I to come between a girl and her nose?", "It's November, yay!" and "Cinnamon hazelnut!" This woman cannot possibly have 545 friends. If she has five, I'd be shocked. So I say unfriend her. Unfriend Gina, unfriend all the Ginas of the world. They're not your friends. Tonight I'm planning to launch a new holiday. Two weeks from today, November 17th will heretofore be known as National Unfriend Day. On National Unfriend Day, I encourage you to cut out some of the friend fat in your life. A friend is someone you have a special relationship with. It's not someone who asks which *Harry Potter* character are you.
So, and then remember five years ago when no one was on Facebook and didn't know what the guy you took high school biology with was having for lunch. Remember how that was ... fine. Let's go back to that. National Unfriend Day. November 17th. Spread the word. And for more on National Unfriend Day, here's William Shatner.
WS Hello, I'm William Shatner. These people on Facebook, they are not your friends.
William Shatner speaking. And let me tell you something about William Shatner, very nice guy, good guy, not my friend.

1.7
a We only just met. She seems nice.
b We've known each other for many years. We get along really well.
c We drifted apart for a few months this year, but now we text each other many times a day and go out every weekend. I know I can rely on JJ.
d His name is Rob. Or Bob? I think.
e I haven't seen Joe in forever, but we email from time to time and I'm going to invite him to my wedding next month. It'll be good to see him again.
f Amy and I have a lot of fun together when we meet. Uh, we're going out on Saturday for some pizza and gossip. I haven't seen her for a while, so we'll have a lot to talk about.

1.8
Mmmmhhh, OK. A: "Does this person give you intense looks?" Wow, he does, too! B: He doesn't hug me that often. Well, not more than other people. Huh! OK ... Now, C: "Have you spent more time together lately?" Have we? Uh ... No, not really. I wish! Next, D: "Is your heart beating faster as you answer these questions?" Can't everybody hear it? Faster and louder! Fine. E: "Do you spend more time with this person than with other friends?" Hmmm. I don't really. I don't ... spend that much time with him. No. OK. F: I do! I do, I do! I love to talk before we go to bed. Now, G: I'm jealous of ... everyone! Hope he is, too, but ... who knows, right? H: "Are you going on holiday together any time soon?" Sadly no. That's it. Let's see what it says here ...

Audio script

▶ 1.9
J = Jake   C = Chloe

J Oh, look at him. He looks quite boring and self-centered.
C Yes, that one definitely is not for me.
J What about this one? They sure do look very sociable.
C Yes, they look fun. And I do like people who are a bit silly. I'll follow them.
J Ah, look at this one. What a cute couple.
C Hmm, yes they certainly are in love. But they're a bit over the top, don't you think? I do hate it when people are like that.
J Ha! Yes, I know what you mean!

▶ 1.10
a So, Lena does seem very smart.
b She certainly does. She's just too knowledgeable for my taste, though.
c How do you like Gamester?
d I do like to relax, but I'm not crazy about online games.
e You certainly aren't.

▶ 1.11
1 What's important to you in a friend?
  I do think we should be like-minded.
2 What do you think about people who post lots of selfies on social media?
  They sure are self-centered, but I don't mind. I like posting them myself.
3 Do you think we use social media too much?
  I do believe we use it a lot, but I don't think it's a problem.
4 What's the best social media app? Why?
  I don't know. I like them all!
5 How can you stay safe online?
  It's definitely important not to share too much information about yourself.

▶ 1.12
a Montagues and Capulets were rival families.
b Romeo and Juliet fell for each other immediately when they met.
c Romeo and Juliet's was an impossible love.
d Good communication is essential in both friendship and love.
e The hardest thing about marriage is learning to communicate with each other.
f When Jo and I met, there was instant mutual attraction between us.
g Respect is the most important thing in any relationship if it's going to last.

h I got a divorce because my ex didn't respect me at all. And he was cheating on me, too.

▶ 1.14
b But Antony cheats on his wife, Fulvia.
  No way! With Cleopatra, right?
c Exactly. He falls for Cleopatra in Egypt.
  So what happens next?
d Back in Rome, his wife dies and he marries Caesar's sister, Octavia.
  Hang on a sec! He marries Caesar's sister?
e He marries her and then goes back to Cleopatra.
  Are you serious? He cheats on her, too?
f He cheats on Caesar's sister, That's right. And then?
g In the end, Antony and Cleopatra die.
  Whoa! What a crazy story!

Unit 2

▶ 2.1
a Yeah! We won't use plastic cups in this office anymore.
  I'm so glad. Those cups take 500 years to decompose.
b What? Three thousand dollars for a couple of solar panels? Forget it!
  Yes, but you will save a lot more money than that on electricity bills.
c Can I have a couple more plastic bags, please?
  Here you are. Would you like to buy a reusable bag?
d It's pretty simple to be eco-friendly. I just try to reuse, reduce, and recycle.
  I know. The three Rs. But it's not so easy!
e What? Recycling? It's useless. Forget it!
  No, it isn't. Think of all the trash you create when you throw things away.
f Are you joking? Why take the stairs when you can take an elevator?
  Because the exercise is good for you and it will save energy.
g I work in the same office as my neighbor, Bill. Sometimes he drives me; other days I drive him.
  Can I join you? That'd make it cheaper for the three of us.

▶ 2.2
a Is the hotel down the road open?
  Yes, I think so.
b Don't go alone. I'll come with you.
  Great! Get your coat.
c Has John gone to the vet?
  Yeah. His dog stopped eating.

d Hey, that's a nice orange top.
  Thanks a lot. I got it at the new store.

▶ 2.3
a In Austria, architects have been building energy-efficient houses.
b Iceland has been using clean electricity from geothermal energy.
c Switzerland has been building national Alpine parks.
d Costa Rica has been planting millions of trees to reduce deforestation.
e Sweden has been using more water and wind power for electricity.
f Norway has been collaborating with Sweden to produce clean energy.
g Brazil has been producing a lot of its fuel from sugar cane.
h In France, more families have been installing solar panels at home.

▶ 2.5
M = Mikaela   L = Lucy

M So, Lucy, which of these do you think is worse?
L That's a tough one. Ummm ... Well, I guess maybe floods. They caused a lot of damage in the city last year.
M Well, yeah, but, you know ... my house wasn't damaged. And Mikaela, your house was OK too, so ...
L Well that's not really the point. I mean, it caused a lot of problems for other people, and, for example, the government still hasn't fixed the old bridge. We still can't use it.
M Yeah, OK, OK. But what about food? I mean the guys in the north have been waiting, what, three, four months for the rain and, you know, all the land is dry and ...
L That's true. But, you know, I think we can solve that problem. Look, I mean, the earth is something like 80% water and ...
M Yeah, OK, but most of that is salt water or ice. You know, we can't just put the ocean on the desert and solve the problem, I mean, that's crazy.
L Ah! Well, that's where you're wrong. Scientists have been working on this and in, like, Israel I think, yeah, in Israel they've been using water from the oceans for many, many years.
M Really? Huh. That's interesting.
L Yeah, so you see, our problem isn't lack of water, like in a drought, it's really having too much water, like in a flood. So, if you look at it like that, floods are a bigger problem. And, you know, a lot of flooding problems are made worse by deforestation and global warming so,

55

Audio script

you know, there are things we can do to help stop flooding and …

▶ 2.8

1 Ready for professional growth? Congratulations! You've won a free online Chinese course. Learn the language that will open doors for intelligent sales people like you. Click here for a free introductory lesson.
2 Your laptop running slow? Clean up tons of junk with Top Clean 3 in 1. 1-click cleaner frees up disk space. Security Plus eliminates harmful files. Performance automatically improves system preferences. Top Clean 3.1 for Mac or Microsoft.
3 Looking for your next professional challenge? Grabowski and Lowe Career Management. Contact us for a confidential discussion: www.gandlcareermanagement.com or call us at 212-555-0988.
4 Want to find a new job? We can help you find the best job to match your strengths. Call Work24/7. Speak to a job expert at 303-555-5546.
5 Tired of commercials? Try soccer streaming. 100% free. Only at livesport.com. High-quality viewing.

▶ 2.9

R = recorded message   C = Cal

1 R Work 24/7! Finding jobs for you whatever you do. Please press one to speak to an expert. Press two … The expert is busy right now. Please leave a message.
  C Hello, Mr. Connie. It's Cal Taylor here. I don't know if you remember me, I came in for an interview a couple of weeks ago. Uh, I'm looking for a job, uh, any job and … Well, look, it's been two weeks and I haven't heard anything from you, or from any potential employers. Your website guaranteed I would only wait a week. I'm going to come into the office tomorrow and I want to talk about this with somebody. Good-bye.

R = recorded message   M = Mia

2 R Hello. You've reached the offices of Grabowski and Lowe, specialists in career advice. We apologize that there is nobody to take your call right now, so please leave a message after the tone.
  M Hi, Ms. Grabowski? Mia Stromboli here. You gave me your card at the conference in Seattle last Thursday. I'd like to arrange an appointment to discuss my career with you at some point. Uh, a little about me. I've been working in the oil industry for 17 years now, both overseas and in the U.S. Uh, I have a lot of management experience and uh … Well, maybe I should tell you this when we meet. So, uh, please call me back at 736-555-8191. Look forward to hearing from you. Bye.

R = recorded message   J = Jake

3 R Welcome to Five Star Chinese courses for professionals. Please press one to order your copy of our book. Press two for a quick language test. Press three to leave a message.
  J Hello? Hello. Yes, uh … Look, I ordered a copy of *Selling in China for Beginners* and, uh, it hasn't arrived yet. Uh, the order number was, uh … Let's see … It was SCB3020. Now, I checked … Oh, my name is Jake Powers. Now, look, I checked my bank account and I paid five weeks ago, so I've been waiting for 35 days. Even with 28 days for delivery, the package is still a week late. Now, I know there were no promises about the mail, but this really isn't good enough. Now, you have my contact details and I want you to call me back before the end of the day so we can figure this out. OK?

▶ 2.10

G = guide   T = tourist   Z = zoo owner

1 G Oh my goodness! Look! There in front of us. I haven't seen one of those for years, they are extremely rare. Oh, isn't he amazing?
  T Is that a … is that … Oh gee! Martha, pass the camera, I'm going to take a photograph.
  G No! Don't open the door. Stay in the Jeep. We're safe in here, he thinks we're one big animal, just like him. If you get out, he might attack you. He can run faster than you think, and that thing on his nose isn't just for decoration.
2 G Shhh! We have to stay very quiet. Just 20 feet in front of me, and up in the trees. I can see … I can see that they're eating fruit, and I don't think they know we're here. Ah! These beautiful golden animals! They are very much at home here in the Brazilian Atlantic forest.
3 Z Hello, and welcome to Zoo Atlanta. Uh, I know you're all very anxious to meet our new arrivals, but, uh, first I'd like to take this, uh, this opportunity to thank our colleagues in China. We have worked very closely with them over a number of years to, uh, to protect this iconic species and to, uh, to reach this success. The mother, Lun Lun, is doing very well and so are the twins.
4 G From our position, here in the helicopter, we can look down and see a fantastic sight. Mother and child traveling along next to each other, completely unaware of us, flying above them. These two will continue their migration along the eastern coast of the United States, from the warm waters in the south to cold feeding grounds of the north.

▶ 2.11

a I'm going to take a photograph.
b I can see that they are eating fruit.
c Hello and welcome to Zoo Atlanta.
d Mother and child traveling along.

▶ 2.12

a Have you ever seen an endangered animal in the wild?
b Have you ever seen one in a zoo?
c Have you ever looked after a sick animal?
d Have you ever given money for an animal cause?
e Have you ever considered working for an animal protection NGO?

▶ 2.13

a Work hard at it and you'll get there.
b What's the point of doing that?
c Keep going. You'll get there in the end.
d If at first you don't succeed, try, try again.
e Do you really think that's a good idea?

▶ 2.14

M = man   W = woman

1 M Oh, I can't believe it! Another "no" letter. This must be the fifth job this month. I'm never going to get a job as a journalist!
  W Hey, listen. You have to believe in yourself. Work hard at it, and you'll get there. I know you can do it!
  M Huh. That's easy for you to say.
2 W Oh, here's my paycheck! Yeah! I've almost saved enough money for my trip!
  M Your trip? What are you talking about?
  W Duh! I've been talking about it, like, forever! Hannah and I are going to take a gap year. We're going to go backpacking and camping across the country and …
  M Wait a minute. You and *Hannah*? Hannah that can't stand spiders? That

Audio script

Hannah? Do you really think that's a good idea?

W Oh come on, she's not that bad. And anyway, it'll be fun.

Unit 3

▶ 3.1

a How do you like your city?
It's a truly awesome city; the city that never sleeps; the capital of the world.

b Is it easy to find your way around?
It is really easy to find your way around because the streets are numbered.

c What's your favorite landmark?
Well, in a city of skyscrapers, I guess it's the Chrysler Building.

d What are the most popular tourist spots?
Central Park, Greenwich Village, 5th Avenue, the World Trade Center, and so many others.

▶ 3.5

a The honking went on for hours until we slowly started moving.

b The firefighters finally opened the door and helped each one of us up to the 15th floor.

c I walked out in my pajamas to get the paper and the wind blew the door shut behind me.

d When we got back to the parking lot, I realized I'd left the keys somewhere.

e Almost 12 hours to buy tickets for a show sounds crazy, doesn't it?

f We couldn't get out because we were between stations.

g The observation deck was so full with people we couldn't get to the door to get down again.

▶ 3.6

a Wow. My whole body hurts.
Well, you hadn't been to the gym in a long time, had you?

b So how did it go last night?
It was just perfect. Chad and me, the music, the lights, everything.

c My neck hurt for a couple of days. And Betty's ears hurt.
That's what a 12-hour trip does to you.

d So what happened in the end?
I told her I was sorry and she accepted my apology. I think we're going to be ok now.

e He asked to see my driver's license.
Did he give you a ticket?

▶ 3.8

a The golden rule is that there are no golden rules.

b Life is short. Break the rules. Forgive quickly. Kiss slowly. Laugh uncontrollably. And never regret anything that makes you smile.

c Know the rules well, so you can break them effectively.

d If you obey all the rules, you miss all the fun.

e You have to learn the rules of the game. And then you have to play better than anyone else.

f There are three rules for writing a novel. Unfortunately no one knows what they are.

Unit 4

▶ 4.1

R = Ruth   D = Dan

R I'm reading this fabulous book about 21st century skills.

D Not another book telling us to teach kids collaboration and creativity, is it?

R Yes, among other important skills. It's a collection of papers by 21 different authors.

D Do any of the authors tell us how to motivate kids to learn reading, writing and arithmetic these days?

R Well, Dan, kids need much more than that to succeed in the 21st century. People need to be able to work together well to solve really complex problems, to show initiative and come up with ideas that have value to others, you know, being creative. Reading, writing, and math are just tools.

D It's all very well for theorists to say that, but how do you keep a group of teenagers engaged in a classroom these days? When everybody is texting everybody, or checking their Facebook timeline, or even gaming during classroom time?

R Precisely! Everyone's connected by technology and, suddenly, that has to stop when they enter a classroom. It's not natural! I really think we are right to use as much information technology in our schools as possible. That's how we prepare kids for a future we can't even imagine. Let them use their cell phones to learn. Let them look for information on the web and share it with everyone in class.

D Let them use their cell phones in class? You can't be serious! How do you know they're not texting their friends?

R Frankly, Dan ... Because you negotiate the rules with your students from the start.

D Fine, let's say they do use their smartphones to look up information for a project. You know as well as I do that the Internet is full of garbage.

R Well, then you teach kids how to find information they can trust. That's a 21st century skill.

▶ 4.2

R = Ruth   D = Dan   C1 = colleague 1
C2 = colleague 2

a R I think schools need to teach 21st century skills.
  C1 Do you think so? I mean, they learn those things at home. School is where they should learn what they can't learn in other places. So, no, I don't agree with you.

b D I believe we should concentrate on reading, writing and arithmetic.
  C2 I don't think so. Well, not only those things. What about art, or history, or music?

c R I think kids have to learn how to solve problems creatively.
  C1 No, I don't think so. They should learn rules, rules, rules.

d R In my opinion, smart phones can be a useful learning tool in class.
  C2 Yeah, you're right. I use them all the time.

e D Smart phones shouldn't be allowed in class.
  C1 Oh, I think so too. They really annoy me. All that beeping.

f D I don't think students should look for information online. It's useless.
  C2 Oh, come on! You think that? The Internet is part of our lives now.

g R Teachers should teach students to find information on the Internet that they can trust.
  C2 That's absolutely right! Yes, I completely agree with you!

▶ 4.7

A
I did something terrible at school once.
Really? What did you do?
I was in 5th grade, I think, and I stuck the teacher's purse to a table.
Why did you do such a thing?
I have no idea. I really don't know.

B
I said something really mean once.
Really? What did you say?

57

Audio script

I looked my mother in the eye and told her that I hated her with all my heart.
What a terrible thing to say!
Yep! I don't really know where that came from.

C
I did the most embarrassing thing a while ago.
Really? What did you do?
This teacher came up to me and there was this insect on her blouse.
So I hit it off with my hand, but it hit the wall and broke into a thousand pieces. And I realized it wasn't an insect. It was some kind of brooch.
Oh no! What a silly thing to do!

▶ 4.9
a If I graduate from college next year, I will look for a job with a tech company.
b If I move to San Francisco, I'll find a good tech job.
c I will be surprised if I find a good job quickly.
d If I won the lottery, I'd travel the world.
e I could write better apps if I had a better computer.
f If I could change one thing about myself, I'd have a smaller nose.

▶ 4.10
a book – could
b blue – two
c could – should
d true – through
e moved – moon
f school – pool
g cook – woman

Unit 5

▶ 5.1
1 I bought a new pair of jeans last week. Do you like them?
2 That's a nice pair of sunglasses. Where did you get them?
3 I really want to buy some new sandals. Where can I get some?
4 So you gave your girlfriend some jewelry for her birthday. Did she like it?
5 I need a suit for my job interview. Where can I get one?
6 I bought a new T-shirt online. Do you like it?

▶ 5.2
A = Andreas   J = Jia
A My bank manager has just approved a 2,000-dollar loan for me.
J I thought you'd applied for three grand.
A I did, but they only approved two grand. I only make 500 bucks a week, you know.
J Did your brother agree to be your co-signer?
A Nope. The good news is my dad agreed.
J Good for him. Do you pay very high interest on the loan?
A 1.5 percent. I guess it's the standard rate for a three-year loan.
J Depends on the terms. When's your first payment due?
A July first.
J Will you be able to pay it off?
A I sure hope so.

▶ 5.3
a If I'd planned my application more carefully, they might have accepted it.
b If I hadn't gone on vacation twice this year, I wouldn't have got into debt.
c If you'd told me, I would have helped you.
d So if she hadn't died, I wouldn't have received it.

▶ 5.6
1 Ladies and gentlemen, we continue boarding American Airlines flight 542 with service to London through gate 37. At this time, we're ready to board passengers in group C. All other passengers, please remain seated. We'd like to invite passengers with "group C" on their boarding passes to board now through gate 37. Please, have your boarding passes ready and passports open at the picture page.
2 Directors, teachers, fellow classmates and families and friends, we are the graduating class of 2014! It is a great honor to be here to commemorate this major moment in my life and that of my fellow classmates. I think we've all been looking forward to today as our prize for the hard work of the last four years.

N = narrator   D = David
3 N In five, four, three, two, one. Ladies and gentlemen, from the top of New York's beautiful Rockefeller Center, we present the *David Perlman Show*. Please welcome your host: David Perlman.
D Good evening everybody. We have a great show for you tonight. Beautiful Miss Taylor Swift and Academy Award winner Jennifer Lawrence are here, ladies and gentlemen.

▶ 5.7
I just spent $3,000 on a designer bag.
$3,000? You can't be serious.
Yeah. And I have another one just like it at home.
Another one? You must be kidding.
I'm not kidding. I bought it last week.
Last week? You must be insane!
Aha. Worse thing is, I feel like buying one more.
One more? You must be out of your mind.
In fact, I'm going there right now.
Right now? You can't seriously expect me to believe that? You must be joking!
You're right. I'm joking.
Ha! I knew it!

▶ 5.9
1 He works as a security guard.
  Security.
2 Don't miss this great opportunity.
  Opportunity.
3 You have completed your transaction.
  Transaction.
4 I got it in an online auction.
  Auction.
5 We will notify you by mail.
  Notify.
6 You have to certify your documents.
  Certify.
7 She's very ambitious.
  Ambitious.
8 That hat is ridiculous.
  Ridiculous.
9 No way. That's unbelievable!
  Unbelievable.
10 Nothing is impossible if you try.
  Impossible.
11 A car suddenly stopped in front of us.
  Suddenly.
12 Luckily, we were wearing seatbelts.
  Luckily.

▶ 5.10
C = customer   SA = sales clerk
C I bought this flash drive yesterday and realized it's only 63 GB instead of the 256 GB I paid for. Can I exchange it for the 256 GB?
SA I just need to see your receipt, please.
C That's the thing. I threw it away, you see.
SA In that case, I'm afraid there's nothing I can do.
C Seriously? But look, I have the bag.

▶ 5.11
C = customer   SA = sales clerk
SA Cash or charge?
C Charge, please.
SA Thank you. Insert your card, please.
C There you go.

Audio script

SA I'm afraid it has been declined.
C I don't understand. Can you try this one?
SA It worked this time. There you are.
C Ah! At last!

 5.12

C = customer   SA = sales clerk

C I like these shoes. Can I try them on?
SA Sure. What size do you wear?
C Size 12.
SA I'm sorry. We're sold out.
C Do you have the same shoe in brown?
SA A size 12 in brown, right?
C Yep. Wait! Forget it. I'm really late as it is. Thanks.
SA You're welcome sir. Good-bye.
C Good-bye.

Unit 6

 6.2

M = man   W = woman

1 M It's the first thing I look at in the morning and the last thing I check at night. I have to know what's happening in the world.
   W Well, I try to limit how much time I spend on it. There is so much information on there that it can take over your life.
2 W Yep, same time every day. I love it. All that drama, the hair and the heavy make-up. Some are very good, too. Great acting, great screenplays, and beautiful locations.
   M Great acting? You must be joking! No way! I have no patience for soaps. The TV networks show them instead of my team, it really annoys me. I love watching my team play.
3 M I'm voting for Jamal, he's pretty awesome on the stage.
   W Totally. Yeah, great voice, but the judges are giving him a hard time.
4 M Love them all, you know? Old episodes of *House*, *Grey's Anatomy*, you name it.
   W Yep, me, too. Weird, though. We're not even doctors.
5 W Can't stand Letterman. Don't like the acid humor. I love Ellen, though ... Ellen DeGeneres?
   M Nope. Never watched Ellen, but come on, Letterman's hilarious.

6.6

Warning!
There is a dangerous virus going around. It's called WORK.
If you receive WORK from your colleagues, boss, or anyone else, via email or any other means, DON'T TOUCH IT UNDER ANY CIRCUMSTANCES!
This virus will destroy your private life completely. If you come into contact with WORK, put on your jacket, take two good friends and get out.
The only antidote is known as EN-TER-TAIN-MENT. You can find it in bars, clubs and movie theaters. Take the antidote repeatedly until WORK has been completely eliminated from your system.
Forward this warning immediately to at least five friends. If you realize that you do not have five friends, this means that you are already infected and that WORK already controls your life.
Remember! It is a deadly virus!

6.7

a Make sure you go home on time.
b Think about taking a vacation somewhere.
c Always have enough water to drink.
d Never try to do more than you can.
e If you take regular breaks, you'll be more efficient.

6.8

L = Lynn   D = Djamilla

L Hi, Djamilla. Hey, I've just been reading a list of things artists want in their dressing rooms, you know, when they perform. They are crazy!
D Yeah! Any good ones?
L Loads. Guess what Beyoncé wants?
D No idea. Flowers? Diet Coke? A huge bathtub?
L No, Bey wants really juicy baked chicken, with fresh garlic, salt, black pepper, and cayenne pepper, you know?
D No way! Like really hot chicken? Maybe it's good for her voice.
L Yeah. Hot babe Bey eats real hot chicken in the dressing room.
D Well, I heard Katy Perry wants a really specific list of crazy stuff.
L Oooohhh! What does California girl want in her dressing room?
D She wants, like ... a modern, glass top dressing room table and uh ... a pair of really ornate French orange floor lamps.
L You're kidding, right? A couple of ornate French lamps!!!
D I know, how crazy is that?
L Shhhhhhh. Listen. I heard Britney Spears used to demand a framed picture of Lady Diana ... mphhhhhh.
D What? You can't be serious. A picture of Lady Diana?
L I swear it's true. Well, at least that's what I heard. Bizarre, right? But not everybody is that crazy. I mean, RiRi only wants Oreo cookies, nothing fancy.
D RiRi? Who's that?
L What! You don't know? That's Rihanna— girlfriend!
D Oh, right! RiRi, cool! So, she only wants cookies? That's sweet.
L I know, right. I guess she can't live without them!
D "It takes me all the way. I want you to staaaay!"
L Woo! Go girl! And you know Adele? She insists that anyone who gets free tickets for her shows has to make a donation to a charity.
D Wow. Free tickets. I wish! Girl, I'd love to see Adele. She's awesome.
L Yeah ... That would be just great.

Unit 7

 7.3

a The check is in the mail.
b You pay this one, I'll pay next time.
c We can still be good friends.
d You look great, Carol!
e Please believe me, Tina, I didn't marry him for his money.
f This has never happened to me before.

7.4

G = Greg   J = Janet

J ... Sure! How can I help you?
G Well, I need to know how to upload music from my computer to my tablet.
J OK. Let's see if I can help you. Uh ... First of all, can you tell me what kind of tablet you have?
G Yes. It's an iPad.
J OK. I wonder if you've installed iTunes on your computer?
G I what? I have no idea what you're talking about, Janet ... I'm not really familiar with software names.
J Oh, dear. Never mind ... Uh ... Do you at least know if you have a Mac or a PC?
G Yes, that I can tell you. I have a MacBook.
J Good, Greg! So you do have iTunes after all! Phew!
G Whatever. Maybe you could now tell me how I can upload music to my tablet?
J Yes, of course, you just ...

 7.5

a Can you tell me ...
b I wonder if ...
c I have no idea if ...

59

Audio script

d I need to know if ...
e Do you know if ...
f Do you have any idea ...
g Could you tell me ...

▶ 7.6
a How old are you?
b Where do you live?
c Do you have a fast car?
d When did you start learning English?
e Can you dance well?
f Who would you take to a desert island?

▶ 7.10
Extract 1
The book's called *The Dumbest Generation* and basically it says that the Internet is making young people stupid.
Well, he has a point.
Seriously Tom?
Yeah, I mean we can't deny that teens are buying fewer books ...

Extract 2
We're not reading as much as people in their 30s or 40s, you know. I mean, book stores like Borders are going out of business week after week. I find that ...
Well, it depends on what you mean by reading. It's ... it's not that teens are reading less.

Extract 3
I don't know, but you see, the point is, reading has been on the decline for ...
Barbara, but don't you think ...
Hold on a second, let me finish. Listen, people have been reading less for at least 30 years, long before the Internet ever existed.

Extract 4
The book says teens are getting dumber. I totally disagree. If anything, people's IQs have gone up, not down, over the past 90 years or so.

Extract 5
That may be true, but don't you think there's something wrong here?

Extract 6
Young people are starting to avoid face to face contact because of the Internet.
Yeah, I couldn't agree more.

Unit 8

▶ 8.1
K = Kate   L = Lily

K So Lily, let's talk about selfies. Do you post them?
L Ha, oh no, no, no. Never.
K What? Never?
L No, you see I'm really camera-shy, I hate it when people take my photo. The problem is, I just never look good in photos.
K Oh, but you're beautiful!
L Ha thanks, no it's not that I don't like the way I look, I just have bad luck with selfies. I never get the right angle, or it comes out with red-eye. Or even worse, I get photobombed by a bird or something! Nope, nope, nope. Not for me.
K You know what I think your problem is?
L What's that?
K You never use filters or anything! I love all the apps you can get to retouch selfies. They're almost all free and they're really good. Nobody can tell they've been photoshopped!
L But that's cheating!
K It's not cheating, it's being creative!
L So I'm guessing you post selfies on social media then, Kate?
K At least twice a day, without fail. It's a bit of a process. First I take lots – and I mean LOTS – of selfies, then swipe through and choose the best one. Sometimes if I can't decide I send a few to my friend to choose the best.
L Wow, really?
K Yes, of course! Then I use a couple of different apps to doctor the image. You know, hide my spots, make my skin smoother, that kind of thing.
L OK ...
K Then finally I post it – the timing is very important. First thing in the morning is best, because people are waking up and look at their phones first thing, so you get more likes.
L Ha, you surprise me Kate! Definitely not for me, though.

▶ 8.3
J = Josh   A = Alicia

K Ah, that was a good day out today, wasn't it?
A Yes, I had a great time. I'm still confused about how that street performer was floating in air, though.
J Ha, well one thing's for sure, he can't have been actually floating!
A Yes, I know, but how did he do it?
J I don't know. He may have had wires connected to his back, holding him up?
A Yes, but connected to what? There was nothing above him. I think he might have had a special frame under his body, hidden by his clothes.
J You think so? It must have been a very strong frame if so.
A Yes, but perhaps it was connected to a heavy base, which he might have hidden under that rug on the ground.
J Ah, yes I see. I think you're right. It must have been that!

▶ 8.5
a She wanted to get a jewel implant in her eye, but they didn't do it.
   She wanted to get a jewel implant in her eye, but she couldn't get it done there.
b She thought of getting a diamond put in her tooth.
c She got a tattoo, but then she broke up with Jason.
d Now she wants to get the tattoo removed as soon as possible.

▶ 8.7
a You're not American, are you?
b It's hot today, isn't it?
c You like soccer, don't you?
d You had an English class yesterday, didn't you?
e The teacher won't give a test this week, will she?
f You'll finish your homework soon, won't you?
g You'd like a coffee now, wouldn't you?

▶ 8.8
a This is a comfortable chair.
b Good communication is very important.
c Exercise is essential if you want to lose weight.
d My new jeans weren't very expensive.
e Counseling can help you deal with insecurity.
f Dude, that girl is obviously in love with you.

▶ 8.9
a I agree! Speaking is more important than reading and writing. But they are both important, too.
b I'm much better at reading than listening and I want to improve. Thanks for the tips!
c I watched two episodes of a TV show online, but I couldn't understand either of them.
d I love listening! But I prefer American accents to British ones. They are easier to understand.
e @Kweli, do you think? I can't understand either of them. I prefer non-native accents like Japanese or German.

Audio script

Unit 9

9.2
1 Lots of locals told me to be extra careful.
2 Got stopped for speeding. Police officer didn't accept bribe. Stupid.
3 Theft is when someone takes something without you knowing.
4 OK. I think I can help you. Theft is when someone takes something from you.

9.3
G = guide   T = tourist

G Welcome to Chicago City Crime Bus Tour. Today, I'm taking you around the city and giving you some of the history, the dark history of this place. And here we are, first stop. OK, you're looking at the site of one of the most famous Chicago legends.
T1 But … but these are just new apartment buildings.
G Uh, yeah, that's right. But right here, on this spot, was the famous Lexington Hotel.
T1 A hotel? But I thought this was a crime tour?
G That's right, uh … it is. OK, let me ask you. Do you know who lived at the Lexington Hotel? Al Capone. That's right! Mr. Crime himself.
T2 Oh, yeah! I've heard about him. And you're telling me he lived in a hotel? A major criminal …
G Well, he had to live somewhere, right? But this wasn't just any hotel. He had secret rooms in there and escape tunnels. He was prepared.
T1 So why didn't the police just go and get him?
G Oh, they tried. I mean, they wanted him for murder, for illegal alcohol, for corruption. He paid all the politicians, you know. And …
T2 So the politicians were protecting him?
G Well … Not all of them. The president Herbert Hoover personally asked for Capone's arrest in 1929. The police finally arrested him in 1931. And do you know what for? It wasn't because he had killed somebody, or for bribery, or because he had robbed a bank or something. No, they arrested him because he hadn't paid tax for many years on his illegal money!

9.5
a Medellín was recently named the world's most innovative city.
b It was judged by eight different criteria.
c Public spaces were created and government programs reached these communities.
d This neighborhood was once considered a dangerous slum.

9.7
M = man   W = woman

M Did you hear about the teenager that was sent to jail for piracy? Peter Jackson, that's his name, I think.
W Oh, yeah? Like what, selling or just downloading stuff for personal use?
M Well, it says here that they found tens of thousands of mostly illegal movies and songs and games on his hard drive—more than 30 GB apparently.
W Whoa! That's a lot, isn't it?
M Oh, yeah. He'll appear in court next Tuesday, and he could get up to five years.
W What? For downloading stuff? That's not fair!
M Well, but it's more than that. Apparently, he had access to an advance copy of ToyStory 4 … He started charging people to download it before it was commercially available and shared the link on reddit.

9.8
W = woman   M = man

W But, honestly, do you? Do you think that's fair?
M What?
W A five-year sentence.
M Well, no, but I think he's got to spend some time in prison—at least a year, maybe. Otherwise, how else is he going to learn?
W Really? Come on. That is so unfair.
M What do you mean? I mean, I'm not saying he should be sentenced to life or anything, but …
W But he's young and he has his whole life ahead of him. And do we really want to put a boy like Peter in the middle of other dangerous criminals? I mean …
M So what exactly are you suggesting? That he should simply be acquitted? Just like that?
W No, of course not. Maybe he should, I don't know, pay a fine—I mean, a huge one—and then do some sort of community service or something. But definitely not go to jail.

9.9
a He joined the American Union army.
b He was registered as killed in action.
c He decided to move to Europe.
d Frank started by writing false pay checks.
e He created an employee ID.
f The FBI approached him.
g He was released just before his 80th birthday.

9.10
One, two, go!
Want to go?
Do you think he loved hot smoking?
Do you think he'll have stopped smoking?
We'll be working tomorrow.
It will be working tomorrow.
It will have been cooked by your mother.
We love beans cooked by your mother.
Wheels, spread across the park.
It will spread across the park.

9.11
P = Phil   S = Sam

P Thank goodness it's Friday. So, what are you doing this weekend, Sam?
S Nothing fun, I'm afraid, Phil. I think I'll be working all the way through.
P Big project, huh?
S Yeah, it's this report for my boss. He just gave it to me and he wants it by Monday lunchtime.
P No way. That's pretty tough, dude.
S Tell me about it. But if I just stay home, hopefully I'll have finished it in time to watch the game on Sunday night.
P Oh, you watching that?
S Of course, man! I wouldn't miss it. I tell you, if the Lakers win, my prayers will have been answered.
P Huh, I didn't know you were a Lakers fan. You learn something every day. Well, I'll be thinking of you when I'm up at the lake.
S Oh yeah? So what are you doing?
P Oh, I've got the kids this weekend. We're going camping. Yep, we'll be sitting around a fire, singing and cooking on the barbecue and you'll be working hard at home. Well, have fun, big guy.
S Yeah, thanks a lot. Have a good weekend, Phil. Take it easy.

9.12
So, have you heard the story about the lawyer and the cigars? Here's how it goes. A lawyer buys a box of very rare, expensive cigars. To protect them, he takes out an insurance policy so that if they are damaged he can receive some money. About a month later he contacts the insurance company to ask for his money because his cigars have disappeared in "a series of very small fires". The insurance company refuses to pay the lawyer and he takes them to court. The judge decides that because the insurance

Audio script

company hadn't specified what kind of fire was unacceptable, they would have to pay. The insurance company pays the lawyer, but then ... they have him arrested for arson, saying that he had deliberately burned his own property to claim the insurance money!

▶ 9.13

1
Y = Yolanda   B = Brad

Y Dude, where were you?
B Hi, Yolanda.
Y But seriously, Brad, you knew today was the class presentation and ...
B Listen, I'm sorry, alright. Just hear me out if ...
Y Go on then. But this better be good.
B Well, you see, I was working on the presentation last night, just doing the final parts, you know ...
Y Right.
B And, so, well ... I was really tired. It was about three in the morning. And ...
Y And? What happened?
B Oh, I'm such an idiot. I just finished everything and well, I was so tired, you see, and I clicked the wrong button. I mean, I didn't save it and ...
Y Brad!
B I know. I'm such an idiot.
Y Yeah you are and why didn't you call me?
B Well, it isn't what you're thinking. I was going to come, I really was. I just kind of ... I overslept.

2
M = Mom   T = Terry

M What the ... what's happened in here?
T Err, hi Mom, I ...
M Terry, what have you been doing? The kitchen is ... it's destroyed!
T Mom, it's not what it looks like. Honestly, it wasn't me.
M Well, if it wasn't you, who was it?
T That's what I'm trying to tell you. I was upstairs, right, and I heard this loud bang and then I heard the cat and I came downstairs.
M Oh, it was the cat, was it? I see. Well, the cat will have to help me clean it up, won't he?
T But, but Mom!

3
M = Mark   L = Leanie

M Hey, Leanie. You got a text message here.
L Thanks. Could you bring my phone?
M Sure. Err, Leanie. Is this Dave, your ex? 'Hi sweetie.' Leanie, what is this?

L What? Oh, right. Honey, don't worry. It's not what it seems. This is Dave my boss, not Dave my ex. And seriously, Mark, you don't need to worry about this Dave. He's like nearly 60 and has two kids and ...
M But 'sweetie'?
L Oh come on. You're overreacting. Anyway, he calls everyone that.

▶ 9.14

a Where will you be living in five years?
  Err, I don't know. I guess I'll still be living in this city somewhere.
b Have you ever been to court?
  No, of course I haven't!
c Does crime worry you?
  It doesn't really worry me too much. I live in a safe neighborhood and I've never been a target.
d Do you watch TV crime dramas?
  Not really, no. They're not my favorite sort of program.
e How could your city be improved?
  I guess it would be better if there was more public transportation at night.

Unit 10

10.1

M = man   W = woman

1 M1 Oh, I just can't stand days like this! Can you?
  M2 What? You mean the meeting?
  M1 Well, yeah, that was a pretty long one, but no. I mean this. All this rain, the gray skies, the cold ... Winter just really depresses me. I can't wait for spring.
  M2 Yeah, but it's good for the garden. And it cleans the city a little.
  M1 Yeah, right.
  M2 Oh, come on, it's not that bad. I mean, when it's like this you can't go out anyway, so it's better to be here at work. I mean, think about it. What else could you be doing?
  M1 Yeah, I guess you've got a point. But still, I wish it would stop raining.

2 W Hey, look! This is where I went to school.
  M Oh, what? That build ... Hey! Look out!
  W Oh! Idiot! Put your lights on! Idiot!
  M Whoa! That was close.
  W What an idiot! How am I supposed to see him at night if he doesn't put his lights on? Grrrr!

M I know. I hate it when people do that. It's so dangerous. The other day I was driving to ...

3 M OK, that's five dollars and 78 cents. Is that everything?
  W1 Uh, yes ... Yes, thank you. Uh ... Here, six.
  M That's great. And 22 for you. Have a nice day!
  W1 Thank you ... Oh, that does annoy me!
  W2 Uh ... What does?
  W1 That! "22 for you! Have a nice day!" What is that about? Really, it's just so ... So fake! I mean, I only want to buy some vegetables and some milk, it's not like we're best friends or anything. I mean, I don't know him, he doesn't know me ... It's just, grrr!
  W2 OK. I think you need to calm down a little. He's just doing his job.
  W1 Ugh, really? It's just too much, it's so ... plastic! Yuck! It's like, imagine if I meet a complete stranger and say ...

▶ 10.3

J = John   B = Bob

1 J Hey Bob. How's your new house project going?
  B Oh! Hi John. Well, we've put the walls up, as you can see. And the windows are coming next week, but it will be a while before we're living in it. But you know, we're getting there little by little.

R = radio   W = woman

2 R ... and it looks like there's heavy traffic again on the major routes downtown, no surprises there. On the interstate roads there are ...
  W Heavy traffic, huh? Don't need to tell me! Oh, this traffic is driving me crazy! I'm sick and tired of it.

M = man   S = Stewie

3 M Hey. What's up Stewie? You look pretty down.
  S Oh, you know ... It's, well, it's Harriet.
  M Oh, I see. So ... Are you guys arguing again?
  S Yeah, kind of.
  M Look man, every relationship has ups and downs.

M = mother   J = Joel

4 M Joel! Joel... Have you cleaned your room yet? Joel! I'm not going to tell you again. Go clean your room before Grandma gets here.
  J Mom! I was playing. I almost beat him that time!

62

Audio script

M Joel, I don't want to hear it. Now, get into your room and don't come out until it's clean. I've told you again and again.

M = mother   S = son

5 M Ah. It's so good to finally have some peace and quiet.
  S Mom! Can I go home and play video games now?
  M Ah …

▶ 10.5
1 You should apologize for saying that.
2 But who's responsible for solving those things?
3 I'm sick and tired of hearing that.
4 She does have a reason for complaining.
5 There are many ways of improving the city.

▶ 10.6
a How long have we been driving now?
  Err, about five hours.
  Man, no wonder I feel tired.
  Well, look, there's a gas station up here. Why don't [beep]. Why don't we stop to have a break?
b Hon, have you seen my keys?
  Yeah, they're where you left them.
  Oh yeah? Where's that?
  On the bedside table.
  Oh yeah. Huh, I don't [beep]. I don't remember putting them there.
c Oh, these stupid hiccups. I've been hiccupping for hours.
  Oh, I'm sorry, I shouldn't laugh.
  Have you [beep]. Have you tried drinking some water? That always works for me.
d Err, Jim, I'm trying to work here.
  Oh, sorry dude.
  Jim, seriously.
  Yeah, OK, sorry.
  Jim, could you [beep]. Could you please stop doing that?
e Lucy, have you seen my new shoes?
  Yes Mom. You know my shoes didn't match my dress, so …
  That's OK. So where are they?
  Err in your closet. I don't remember.
  Lucy, please [beep]. Please try to remember, I need them now.

▶ 10.7
1 What's wrong? Are you sick?
  Ugh, I think I'm coming down with the flu.
2 I just don't know how to use this software.
  Let me see. I'm sure we can figure it out together.
3 Wow, you look great!
  Aw thanks! You always know how to lift me up.
4 Oh no, I failed my driving test!
  Don't let it bring you down. You can always take it again.
5 Clara always tells me what to do.
  You shouldn't let her boss you around like that.
6 I really wanted to stay in last night, but then John called and …
  No, really? Don't let him change your mind! Decide what you want and stick to it!
7 Why aren't you speaking to Lisa?
  Oh, we fell out last weekend and had a fight.
8 Do you like your brother?
  Oh yes, I get along well with him.

▶ 10.9
Sentence a. Ready? I told her it was difficult and asked her to help me.
Oh yes. 'Told her.' Not 'told to her.'
Next one. A lot of new hotels are being built in my city.
Are being built? Being built? OK.
It started raining soon after we left the house.
That's OK!
My dad complains about getting up early in the morning.
Oh! About getting.
I can't remember where my car is.
Oh! Where my car is.
Where did you get your eyes checked?
Hey, that one's correct!
Can you tell me who wrote this song?
That one's correct, too!
How long have you been living in this city?
Have you been living in this city?
He was awarded an Oscar for his role in the movie.
Correct!
She works as a secretary for a company that specializes in import / export.
She works 'as' a secretary, not 'like' a secretary.

▶ 10.10
a I find it easy to read in English but a little boring.
  You should consider reading things you're interested in.
b I'm not so good at remembering new words.
  Have you thought about keeping a notebook for new words?
c I have a lot of difficulty pronouncing 'sh' and 'ch'.
  A good way of improving your pronunciation is recording yourself.
d Listening is very hard.
  Try to focus on the stressed words.
e It's difficult to speak without pausing a lot.
  How about learning some common phrases like 'I mean' or 'You know'?

Answer key

Unit 1

1.1

1 a 3 b 2 c 1 d 1 e 2 f 3 g 2

2 a How many Facebook friends do you have / ~~you~~?
   b Who makes you laugh most? / ~~do~~
   c What are you really good at? / ~~on~~
   d What makes you nervous? / ~~are~~
   e What did you do last vacation? / ~~does~~
   f Would you like to go to a speed-friending event? / ~~to~~
   g What's something you just can't live without? / ~~do~~

3 a 6 b 7 c 5 d 4 e 3 f 2 g 1

1.2

1 Love Story 1: in, get, apart
   Love Story 2: along, for, They got, got
   Love Story 3: out, for, in, on, up, back

2 a 2 b 3 c 1

3 (8) Romeo dies, (6) escape, (1) meet, (9) Juliet dies, (7) get married secretly, (4) find out their families are enemies, (3) fall for each other, (2) get along well, (5) realize their love is impossible

4 Personal answers.

6 a They meet at a party and get on well immediately.
   b Their love is impossible but also irresistible.
   c The friar marries them secretly.
   d ... but they can't stay together.

1.3

1 a people you can count on.
   b people you are usually in contact with.
   c people you get along with and hang out with.
   d the people you can always rely on.

2 International UnFriend Day is a day for removing unnecessary people from Facebook.

3 helps you move house / has seen you recently

4 on, out, along, from, about, with

5 a acquaintances
   b very close friends
   c very close friends
   d acquaintances
   e friends
   f friends

6 Personal answers.

7 a Y b N c N d Y e N f Y g Y h N
   She should try a bit harder.

1.4

1 1 c 2 f 3 b 4 g 5 a 6 a 7 f 8 h 9 e 10 d

2 Personal answers.

3 definitely is / sure do look / really do like / certainly are / do hate

5 1 c 2 d 3 a 4 e 5 b

1.5

1 a Friendship b Love c Love d Love
   e Nothing f Nothing g Love
   h Friendship i Nothing j Nothing

2 b ADV c ADJ d N e V f N g N h V

3 1 Antony cheats on his wife, Fulvia.
   2 Fulvia dies and Antony goes back to Rome.
   3 Antony marries Caesar's sister, Octavia.
   4 Antony goes back to Egypt and Cleopatra.
   5 Caesar and Antony fight to control Egypt.
   6 Antony and Cleopatra both die.

Unit 2

2.1

1 Not use regular electricity.

2 a F b F c T d F e F f T

3 a G (cups in this) b NG (for a couple)
   c NG (Can I have) d G (simple to be)
   e NG (Forget it) f NG (take an elevator)
   g G (in the same)

4 1 b 2 a 3 d 4 e 5 g 6 f 7 c

5 a pet-friendly b energy-efficient
   c fuel-efficient d reusable e rechargeable

6 b Do you ever practice flexitarianism?
   c Do you have energy-efficient light bulbs at home?
   d Have you walked or cycled to work lately instead of using private transportation?
   e Do you turn off appliances when you're not using them?
   f Do you use eco-friendly cleaning products?
   g Have you changed from plastic to reusable cloth bags?

7 a (hotel, road, open, so) b (Don't, go, alone, coat) c (John, gone, dog, stopped) d (orange, top, lot, got)

2.2

1 2 I haven't been taking taxis
   3 I haven't been using plastic bags
   4 I've been ordering drinks without a plastic straw
   5 I've been eating less red meat and dairy

2 a Proud.
   b Wind and rain.
   c He is saving money.
   d It fills the seas and damages wildlife.
   e He feels more healthy.
   f Personal answer.

3 a Austria
   b Iceland
   c Switzerland
   d Costa Rica
   e Sweden
   f Norway
   g Brazil
   h France

4 a The office **has** been really busy. We've been **working** like crazy.
   b I like your shoes. I've been trying **to** find a pair like that **since** last year.
      OR I **was** trying **to** find a pair like that last year.
   c So sorry! Have you been **waiting** for long?
   d Hey! I've been trying to call you **since** yesterday. Where **were** you?
      OR I **was** trying to call you yesterday.
   e He's been **studying** English for **years**.
      OR ... English for **a** year.
   f They've been playing soccer.
      OR They **were** playing soccer before.
   g Joan**'s / has** been managing **the advertising company** since 2012.

2.3

1 a POACHING
   b DROUGHTS
   c FLOODS
   d DEFORESTATION
   e RISING SEA LEVELS
   f DUMPING OF E-WASTE
   g THREATENED SPECIES
   h FOSSIL FUELS
   i CLIMATE CHANGE

2 Floods, droughts, deforestation, global warming.

3 a Floods.
   b No.
   c No.
   d 3 or 4 months ago.
   e 80%.
   f Israel.

4 a have replaced b have eliminated / have been planting / has planted c has developed / has dropped d have stopped / have become e have been trying

5 a How long have you known your best friend?
   b Have you been working hard recently?
   c Have you ever lived in a different city?
   d How long have you been studying today?
   e How much bread have you eaten today?
   f How far have you walked today?
   g How many cups of coffee have you drunk today?
   h Have you been exercising a lot lately?

2.4

1 a 4
   b 5
   c 3
   d 1
   e 2

2 See ▶2.8.

3 a **Are you** ready for professional growth?
   b **Is your** laptop running slow?
   c **Are you** looking for **your** next professional challenge?
   d **Do you** want to find a new job?
   e **Are you** tired of commercials?

4 a M b J c J d C e M f C

5 a came
   b 's been / haven't heard
   c 've reached
   d 've been working
   e ordered / hasn't arrived
   f checked / paid / 've been waiting

6 a I started this course in February.
   b I've had my job for five years.

Answer key

c Our teacher gave us lots of homework last week.
d I've learnt 10 new words this lesson.
e I didn't go out last night.

2.5

1 1 Javanese rhino 2 Golden lion tamarin
3 Giant panda 4 North Atlantic right whale

2 a I'm going to take a photograph.
b I can see that they are eating fruit.
c Hello and welcome to Zoo Atlanta.
d Mother and child travelling along.

3 a Have you ever seen an endangered animal in the wild? / a
b Have you ever seen one in a zoo? / a
c Have you ever looked after a sick animal? / on
d Have you ever given money for an animal cause? / never
e Have you ever considered working for an animal protection NGO? / it

4 33%, 10%, nearly 0%

5 a Work hard at it and you'll get there. (E)
b What's the point of doing that? (D)
c Keep going. You'll get there in the end. (E)
d If at first you don't succeed, try, try again. (E)
e Do you really think that's a good idea? (D)

6 Person 1 wants to get a new job (phrase a).
Person 2 wants to take a gap year (phrase e).

Unit 3

3.1

1
Across	Down
4 smoggy	1 chaotic
6 upscale	2 fashionable
7 polluted	3 neglected
	5 rundown
	8 lively

2 a fashionable b rundown c polluted
d chaotic e smoggy f lively

3 a How do you like your city?
  a / the / the / the
b Is it easy to find your way around?
  the
c What's your favorite landmark?
  a / the
d What are the most popular tourist spots?
  the
They are talking about New York City.

3.2

1 a T b F c T d N e T f T

2 a had told b had sent c had made
d had kissed e hadn't hugged
f had mistaken g had shaken h had broken

3 a Did you know the Romans **spoke** Latin?
b After we **arrived** home, we made some sandwiches.
c By the time we got home, the TV show **had** finished.
d When I had **had** lunch, I had a short nap.
e We **bought** our car five years ago.

4 a gone b been c been d been

5 a Hi, this is your travel host.
b I'd like to show you the top ten attractions of Madrid, Spain.
c Number ten. Plaza de Cibeles. Madrid is known for many beautiful squares like this one.
d The Cibeles fountain is an important symbol of this city.
e Number nine. Almudena Cathedral. It took more than a hundred years to complete its construction in 1993.
f The original site was occupied by Madrid's first mosque.

3.3

1 Carlos driving. Anya crime. Mike noise. Margaret money.

2 1 traffic
2 spot
3 theft
4 vandalism
5 pickpocketing
6 rate
7 honking
8 noise
9 debt
10 balance

3 1 d 2 g 3 a 4 h 5 c 6 j 7 i 8 b
9 f 10 e

4 a car theft
b suffer from loneliness
c work–life balance
d be in debt
e find a parking spot
f constantly connected

5 Personal answers.

3.4

1 a wonder
b turn
c mean
d poor
e joking

2 c, a, f, b, d, g, e

3 a had been doing exercise
b had been dancing
c had been flying
d had been fighting
e had been speeding

4 a had been hanging out
b had made / had been making
c had gotten
d had been dating
e had killed

5 a I had to sit down because I'd been standing all day.
b We got lost because we hadn't understood the directions.
c OK
d Vera had visited Turkey before so she knew the best places.
e Until yesterday night, I had never eaten meat before.
f OK
g How long had you been waiting when the doors opened?

3.5

1 a 5 b 1 c 3 d 6 e 2 f 4

2 a Danger! No lifeguard **on** duty.
b Kindly refrain **from** smoking.
c Park here **at** your own risk.
d Please clean **up** after your pet.
e Tow **away** zone. Do not stop here.
f Vehicles will be towed **at** owner's expense.

4 f, c, e, a, d, b

Unit 4

4.1

1 literature, art, geography, math, history, languages, chemistry, physics, biology

2 a R b D c R d R e D f D g R

3
Agree	Disagree
e	b, c
g	a
d	f

5 Do: badly, an exercise, homework, well
Get: feedback, good grades, into trouble, kicked out, a report card
Make: a difference, mistakes, progress
Take: an exam, photos, a test

6 1 e 2 f 3 b 4 a 5 g 6 c 7 d

4.2

1 b too much c too many d never enough
e too much f too much g too little
h no / too many i too much

2 a rich
b problems
c noise

4 walking to school / windy / Thursday / a café

4.3

1 Personal answers

2 1 b 2 c 3 a

3 b ... worked harder.
c ... chosen art.
d ... have dressed appropriately for the interview.
e ... gone to music school when I had the chance.
f ... have dropped out of college.

5 a 2, 3, 5, 4, 1
b 3, 2, 5, 1, 4
c 4, 5, 1, 3, 2

6 a do b say c do

4.4

1 1 d 2 f 3 a 4 c 5 b 6 e

2 a will look for
b move
c will be
d won
e had
f could

3 first conditional: a, b, c
second conditional: d, e, f

65

Answer Key

4 /uː/ blue, two, true, through, moved, moon, school, pool, new
/ʊ/ book, could, push, should, would, put, pull, cook, woman

4.5

1 1 a, an, the, an, the, a, the, The
2 a, the, the, The, a, the, the
3 a, the, the, a, the, The, the

2 a Two
b *Gifted* and *Magnus*
c *Gifted*
d *Hidden Figures*

3 a What's done is done. (S)
b What were you thinking? (C)
c It's not the end of the world. (S)
d You should've known better. (C)
e How could you do such a thing? (C)
f Don't let it get you down. (S)
g Will you ever learn? (C)

5 b You should've studied for the test.
If you'd studied for the test, you wouldn't have failed.
c You shouldn't have been absent a lot.
If you hadn't been absent a lot, you wouldn't have got bad grades.
d You shouldn't have cheated on a final exam.
If you hadn't cheated on a final exam, you wouldn't have been kicked out of school.
e You should've got into college.
If you'd got into college, your parents wouldn't have been upset.

Unit 5

5.1

1 1 c 2 e 3 a 6 f (*b* and *d* are not used.)

2 1 free Wi-Fi, charging stations, virtual try-ons
2 coupons, in-store shopping
3 self-checkout, user-generated content, brand loyalty

3 [crossword with: SUNGLASSES, SCARF, JEANS, BIKINI, JEWELRY, PANTS, etc.]

4 a sunglasses, jeans, pants, sandals, shorts, earrings, shoes
b sunglasses, jeans, pants, sandals, shorts, earrings, shoes, jewelry
c scarf, bikini, sweater, jacket, T-shirt, suit, bag

5 1 Do you like them?
2 Where did you get them?
3 Where can I get some?
4 Did she like it?
5 Where can I get one?
6 Do you like it?

5.2

1 1 off / back 2 on 3 out 4 out, into

2 1 T$3,000
2 $500 a week
3 his father
4 1.5 %
5 July 1st

3 a might
b hadn't
c have
d wouldn't

5

Silent *b*	Silent *t*	Silent *gh*	*gh* = /f/
doubt	fasten	bought	enough
thumb	listen	though	laugh

6 a bought
b Fasten
c thumb
d listen / laugh
e doubt / enough / though

5.3

1 a your clothes / your money / your name
b your money / your chair / your word
c your hair / a hairdryer / a towel
d the letter *e* / the letter *s* / the letter *m*
e food / poison / nothing

2 1 d 2 c 3 e

3 1 c 2 e 3 a 4 b 5 f 6 d

4 You must: be insane, be joking, be out of your mind
You can't: seriously expect me / us to believe that

5 can't be serious, must be joking, must be insane, must be out of your mind, can't seriously expect me to believe that

5.4

1 a, c, b, d

2 Only the Hollywood sign.

3

Nouns		Verbs
security	transaction	notify
opportunity	auction	certify

Adjectives		Adverbs
ambitious	unbelievable	completely
ridiculous	impossible	luckily

4 a secure
b marvelous
c disappointment
d washable
e nicely
f purify

5 a OK
b kind, old
c gorgeous, shiny
d OK
e lovely, big

5.5

1 c

2 a near
b difficult
c slowly
d after
e most expensive
f price per unit

3 c, b, a, e, f, d
SC, C, C, SC, C, C

4 Cash, Insert, card, afraid, declined

5 See ▶ 5.12.

Unit 6

6.1

1 What Makes Today's Series More Addictive Than Ever Before?

2 a have / using b having c has d are e told
Correct sequence according to paragraphs of the text: c, e, d, b, a.

3 a to (T)
b of (F)
c than (T)
d for (F)
e on (F)

4 a sports events
b medical drama
c reality TV
d TV streaming services
e soap opera
f talk show
g music program
h social media

5 1 h 2 e/a 3 c 4 b 5 f

6.2

1 a The / in / of (F)
b The / of (T)
c The / in (F)
d of (T)
e a / of (T)
f of / the / on (F)

2 a The contestant **who is** leaving the island this week is Fifi. / *Survivor*.
b The women who **live** in the house want to get married. / *The Bachelor*.
c The island **that** we chose is very beautiful. / *Survivor*.
d Sally baked a cake in the shape of Spider-Man, **which was** inspired by the superhero. / *The Great British Baking Show*

3 a Nicki Minaj and Mariah Carey are judges whose fights on camera were popular on Twitter.
b Catherine is the girl who / that won the diamond engagement ring.
c The location that the organizers choose is usually far away from civilization.
d Simon Cowell is a reality TV producer whose shows include *American Idol* and *The X Factor*.

66

Answer Key

e Kim's the woman who / that won after the other 14 contestants left the island.
f He's chosen a song that is close to his heart.
g The dances that the professionals teach them can be difficult.

4 1 that
2 who
5 that
7 that

5 a 6 OK
b 1 Every week. Botafogo, which is the best team in Brazil, play in the top league.
c 3 Definitely. I hate all the actors who / that are fake.
d 7 I don't think shows which / that have violence should be on in the daytime.
e 4 OK
f 5 OK
g 2 OK

6.3

1 b 2 d 3 f 4 a 5 g 6 c e is extra

2 ... , **whose** universe includes ... /, **which** has made ... / **that** / **which** has reached every corner of the planet / ... , **who** created and directed most of the movies / .... , **whose** novels sold millions of copies to all age groups / ... , **which** were mainly written in a cafe, / **that** / **which** she created.

3 **Spider-Man:** Spider-Man, who was originally a Marvel superhero, has had six movies. (N) The fourth one premiered in 2017 with a cast that included a new Spider-Man played by Tom Holland. (R)
Mary Jane Parker, who was the love interest between 2002 and 2007, was cut from the 2012 and 2014 movies. (N)
The Hunger Games: Author Suzanne Collins, whose novels inspired four movies, must be pretty pleased with the amazing success of *The Hunger Games* saga. (N)
These exciting movies, which have captivated young adults worldwide, tell the story of a compulsory death match. (R)
It's a televised match that the contestants must win in order to survive. (R)

4 a *The Dark Knight* / which is my favorite Batman movie / won four Oscars.
b Heath Ledger / who played the scariest Joker ever seen / won an Academy Award after he died.
c Christian Bale / who played Batman / wasn't nominated for an Oscar for his part.
d This sentence doesn't have speech pauses, because it is a restrictive relative clause.
e *Pirates of the Caribbean* / which was inspired by Disneyworld's attraction / has made over five billion dollars so far.

6.4

1 a prequel
b clip, views
c trilogies
d cast
e shoot, script

2 a It's called work.
b No, in any circumstances.

c It can destroy your private life completely.
d It's entertainment.
e Bars, clubs, and movie theaters.
f At least five friends.
g It means you're already infected and work already controls your life.

3 a Make sure you go home on time.
b Think about having a vacation somewhere.
c Always have enough water to drink.
d Never try to do more than you can.
e If you take regular breaks, you'll be more efficient.

4 1 Really? You're kidding, right?
2 No way! Thank goodness!
3 Are you serious?
4 What? Get out of here!

6.5

1 a F b T c F d T e T

2 a

3 a baked
b furnished / specific
c pair / French lamps
d picture of
e short / eat
f an Adele / you must

Unit 7

7.1

1 Be active in promoting it.

2 1 calm
2 find
3 take
4 goes
5 pick
6 setting
7 break
8 cut

3 a distance learning
b movie streaming app
c video conferencing
d screen time
e online selling platform
f identity theft

4 1 b 2 a 3 e 4 c

7.2

1 1 tell 2 say 3 tell 4 tell 5 tell 6 tell 7 say 8 tell 9 say 10 say

2 a 3 b 5 c 1 d 4 e 2

3 1 we were nearly there
2 my picture was brilliant
3 there was no more ice cream left
4 they were leaving without me
5 we'd come back and buy it next time

4 a was
b he would
c we could
d she looked
e she didn't marry / she hadn't married
f had, him

5 Mark told Anna he would marry her. / Mark said he would marry Anna. Anna said / told Mark (that) she had never been interested in marriage. Mark told Anna he knew she loved him. / Mark said he knew (that) Anna loved him.
Anna told Mark that she couldn't marry him. Anna told Mark she was in love with someone else.

7.3

1 b

2 a, b, c, e, g

3 a Can you tell me ...
b I wonder if ...
c I have no idea if ...
d I need to know if ...
e Do you know if ...
f Do you have any idea ...
g Could you tell me ...

4 b you have installed iTunes on your computer.
c I have no idea what you're talking about.
d I need to know if you're familiar with the different icons.
e Do you know if you have a Mac or a PC?
f Do you have any idea when you bought it?
g Could you tell me how I can upload music to my tablet?

5 b where I live.
c if I have a fast car.
d when I started learning English.
e if I can dance well.
f who I would take to a desert island.

6 /ʊ/ pull, push, put, cushion, notebook, full
/ʌ/ plug, button, cut, under, comfortable, shut, bug

7.4

1 b What did you do
c Do you like
d will you finish
e Are you
f has your / improved

2 a Sue asked me **not to** call her tonight.
b I asked her where **she was** going.
c She asked me why **I wanted** to know.
d I told her **not to** be rude to me.
e She **told** me to leave her alone.

3 a Q b R c Q d Q e R f Q g Q h R

4 e, b, d, f, c, g, a

5 a F b T c T d T e F

7.5

1 a social networking
b visiting museums
c studying for class
d leisure reading
e playing video games
f watching online movies

2 Personal answers.

3 e, a, c
(suggested answers)
b + ppl text than call
d Libraries – customers now
f games + common smartphone use < 15 yrs

67

Answer Key

4 1 A: We can't deny that robots will do all our jobs in the future.
B: I totally disagree. There are some jobs only humans can do.
2 A: That guy on the TV is speaking nonsense.
B: Well, you may agree or disagree, but he makes some valid points.
3 A: No, they don't think ...
B: Hold on a second, let me finish.
4 A: Translation technology nowadays is excellent.
B: Yeah, I couldn't agree more.
5 A: I think teens spend too much time on the Internet.
B: That may be true, but don't you think there are some benefits to it?
6 A: Well, it depends what you mean by "advantages".
B: My point exactly!

5 a It depends on what you mean by... / of
b Hold on a second, let me finish. / in
c We can't deny that... / to
d That may be true, but... / is
e I couldn't agree more. / be
f I totally disagree. / am

6 1 c 2 a 3 b 4 f 5 d 6 e

Unit 8

8.1

1 photo 1 Lily photo 2 Kate

2 a F b T c F d T e T f T

3 a shy b red c photobombed
d retouch e photoshopped f doctor

4 c

5 a F b T c T d F e F
Personal answer.

8.2

1 1 d 2 c 3 a 4 e 5 b

2 a must have come
b can't have been
c must have won
d might have overslept
e can't have seen

3 Personal answer.

4 Personal answer.

5 a can't have been
b may have had
c might have had
d must have been
e might have hidden

8.3

1 3, 2, 1
too expensive = teeth; not available where she lives = eye; did it but regrets it = tattoo

2 a implant in her eye, but they didn't do it / she couldn't get it done there.
b a diamond put in her tooth, but she couldn't afford it.
c a tattoo, but then she broke up with Jason.
d wants to get the tattoo removed as soon as possible.

3 a D b F c D d D e F f T g T

5 Personal answers.

6 Personal answers.

8.4

1 Across
1 nightstand 3 bookcase 5 chair
7 mirror 8 pillow 10 double bed
Down
2 dresser 4 comforter 5 closet 6 lamp
9 rug

2 a More
b many
c are

3 1 bed 2 bed 3 ceiling 4 floor 5 desk
6 lamps 7 desk 8 desk 9 bed 10 floor

4 a are you? ↘ b isn't it? ↘ c don't you? ↘
d didn't you? ↗ e will he / she? ↗
f won't you? ↗ g wouldn't you? ↘

8.5

1 a Open your ears
b More than the language
c Guessing is good
d Don't be afraid!

2 a Songs, streamed TV shows, podcasts.
b Living abroad is expensive.
c ... learn about the culture behind the language.
d ... learn to focus on the words you know and trust your guesses for the ones you don't
e Any two of: Everybody will be pleased that you are trying / the better you'll feel / the more you'll want to learn / the quicker you will improve

3 a comfortable
b communication
c essential
d expensive
e insecurity
f obviously

4 a both / ... more important **than** reading and writing.
b better / ... and I want **to** improve.
c either / ... but I couldn't **understand** either of them.
d to / They are **easier** to understand.
e either / ... ... I **prefer** non-native accents ...

Unit 9

9.1

1 a a bribe
b to kidnap
c to go to prison
d to steal

2 1 5
2 6
3 4
4 3

3 1 Lots of locals told me to be extra careful.
2 Got stopped for speeding. Police officer didn't accept bribe. Stupid.
3 Theft is when someone takes something without you knowing.
4 OK, I think I can help you. Theft is when someone takes something from you.

4

Crime	Criminal	Verb
bribery		to bribe (sb)
burglary	a burglar	to break into (a house)
drug dealing	a drug dealer	to deal drugs
kidnapping	a kidnapper	to kidnap (sb)
murder	a murderer	to murder / kill (sb)
robbery	a robber	to rob (person / place)
theft	a thief	to steal (sth)

5 b Bribery
c have kidnapped
d organized crime
e robbery
f stole

6 a He's Al Capone.
b He lived in a hotel.
c The president of the U.S. at the time.
d He was arrested because he hadn't paid tax for many years on his illegal money.

7 a are looking
b Do / know
c 've heard
d hadn't paid

9.2

1 a Medellín was recently named the world's most innovative city. / of
b It was judged by eight different criteria. / were
c Public spaces were created and government program reached these communities. / was
d This neighborhood was once considered a dangerous slum. / by

2 1 ⊕ 2 ⊖ 3 ⊕ 4 ⊕ 5 ⊖ 6 ⊕

3 1 was 2 am 3 was 4 is 5 is 6 has been
5 is not passive voice.

4 a 2 b 4 c 1

5 a An alternative system **was developed**. It's **considered** a success.
b Curitiba's bus system **is often compared** to an underground railway, Curitiba's buses **are used** by its 2.3 million residents.
c The BRT system **has been adopted** in / by 83 cities worldwide. **It will soon be implemented** by the Canadian government.

9.3

1 NY teen arrested for selling movie before official release date

2 a F b F c T d T

3 be acquitted   (N)
do community service   (W)
pay a fine   (W)
be sentenced to life   (N)
be sentenced to one year in prison   (M)

Answer Key

4 1 c 2 a
5 a B b A c B d B e F f F
7 a under b on c on d for e of

9.4

1 2 1
4 3
5 6
8 7
10 9
2 Let it expire before you renew it., ~~Try using your name and birthday—nobody will guess that!~~, ~~Don't use the Internet at home.~~
3 a Hotspot / *hotspot*
b Track / *track* (any verb form)
c Up-to-date / *up-to-date*
d Target / *target*
e Password / *password*
f Click / *click*
4 a You can make your computer more secure **by** using virus protection software.
b The last guests had arrived **by** 10:00 p.m.
c The malware was uploaded **by** some hackers.
d I'll be home **by** midnight.
e Tony improved a lot **by** working hard.
5 a F b F c T d T   Sam is man A.
6 a 'll be working
b wants it by
c I'll have
d will have been
7 a won't have / won't be having fun
b won't have finished the report by / won't finish the report on
c will see / is seeing / is going to see / will be seeing his children

9.5

1 c
2 4 1
5 3
2
3 1a, 2d, 3b
4 a F b T c F d F e F f F
5 a 9.4 Where will you be living in five years' time?
b 9.3 Have you ever been to court?
c 9.1 Does crime worry you?
d 9.5 Do you watch TV crime dramas?
e 9.2 How could your city be improved?

Unit 10

10.1

1 a 3 b 4 c 5 d 1 e 2
The Malcolm X quote sees anger as a positive emotion.
2 seldom, bring about, complaining
3 1 weather 2 bad drivers 3 insincerity
4 a T b F c T d F e F f F
6 1 b 2 c 3 a 4 e 5 d

10.2

1 1 Car modifications
2 Chewing gum
3 Eating on public transportation
2 a 3 b 2 c 1 d 1 e 3
3 a for making
b Stopping
c meeting
d throwing
e listening
f of complaining
4 a A b D c D d A e D c D
5 a should apologize for saying that,
b responsible for solving those things
c sick and tired of hearing
d have a reason for complaining
e There are many ways of

10.3

1 a for b of c about d about e of f for
g about
2 a stopped to ask for directions / stopped asking for directions
b tried opening the door / tried to open the door
c remember to visit my grandparents / remember visiting your grandparents
d stopped to buy milk / stopping buying milk
3 is played, lives, is ordered, broke, lost, is visited, have destroyed, didn't believe
4 a Why don't we stop to have a break?
b I don't remember putting them there.
c Have you tried drinking some water?
d Could you please stop doing that?
e Please, try to remember.

10.4

1 a myself b myself c myself d yourself
e themselves f yourself g themselves
2 1 c 2 g 3 a 4 f 5 b 6 h 7 d 8 e
3 1 c coming down with
2 e figure it out
3 g lift me up
4 a bring you down
5 f boss you around
6 h stick to it
7 b fell out
8 d get along well with

10.5

1 a 3 b 5 c 1 d 2 e 6 f 4
2 a I told **her** it **was** difficult and asked her to help me.
b A lot **of** new hotels are **being built** in my city.
c OK
d My dad complains **about getting** up early in the morning.
e I can't remember where **my car is**.
f OK
g OK
h How long **have you been living in** this city?
i OK
j She works **as** a secretary for a company **that** specializes in import / export.

3 1 find / to read
2 at remembering
3 difficulty
4 Listening
5 It's
4 1 d You should **consider reading** things you're interested in.
2 e Have you **thought** about **keeping** a notebook for new words?
3 a A good way of **improving** your pronunciation **is recording** yourself.
4 b Try **to focus** on the stressed words.
5 c How about **learning** some common phrases like "I mean" or "you know"?
5 Personal answers.

69

Phrase Bank

This Phrase Bank is organized by topics.
▶ The audio is on the ID Richmond Learning Platform.

Getting to know people

Unit 1
Do you have any nicknames?
Are you usually more optimistic or pessimistic?
What's the first thing you notice when meeting someone new?
Where are you and your family from?
What are the three most important objects you have at home?
What did you want to be when you were a kid?
Which sports team do you and your family support?
What do you do to wake yourself up in the morning?
I don't know. Maybe join a sports club or take a course.
I guess one advantage is that you get to know a lot of different people.

Relationships

Unit 1
Have you met all your classmates?
Yes and no. I mean, I've seen them, but I haven't spoken to them all yet.
My sister broke up with her boyfriend last year, but they got back together after a week.
Oh yeah? Are they still together?
Taylor Swift and Calvin Harris broke up in 2016.
I'd never fall for someone who likes pop music – I can't stand it!
Justin Bieber met Selena Gomez in 2009 after his manager called her mom to arrange a meeting.
They dated on and off for years, but they finally broke up in 2018.
We've known each other since elementary school. We used to be really close.
I have a lot of very close friends.

Asking for and giving opinions

Unit 1
I think selfies show that someone cares a lot about what they look like.
I post a lot of group photos, but I definitely don't feel lonely!
My brother is always posting selfies, and he's incredibly self-centered.
I do believe that …
People seem to …
I do agree that …
I definitely think that …

Unit 2
I'd never try the Moringa stuff. I don't believe in all these "superfoods".
Hmm … maybe I'd go to the retreat. I need a rest.

Unit 3
I feel most sorry for … because …
Our city has a lot of problems. I love it, though.
Really? I don't. I'm tired of living here.
How do you feel about …?
What do you think of …?

Unit 4
And I think uniforms are a good idea. It's one less decision to make in the morning.
No way! I love wearing my own clothes.

Reactions / Listening actively

Unit 1
You mean the date?
Go on.
Hold on a sec.
No way!
What happens next?
What do you mean "leaves"?
Are you sure?
Oh, dear!
So, I finish work and I'm walking to my car. I'm tired and really looking forward to getting home. I open …
Uh-huh. Yeah. And then …?

Unit 3
What do you mean?
You poor thing! Oh, no!
You're joking! Gee! And how did it turn out?
No wonder!
I was going to visit my grandparents once, and we got stuck on the highway for four hours.
Oh, no. You poor thing. What happened?
So, I was going for a job interview, I'd been looking for a job as an architect for ages, so I was really nervous.
Well, it was my cousin's birthday, and I'd been planning …
Well, I'm sure something better will come along …
What do you mean I can't park here? Says who?

Unit 4
Really? What did you do?
Why would you say such a thing?

Going green

Unit 2
Well, 1 is plastic bottles. I think it takes a lot of energy to produce them.
Yes, and then the oceans are full of plastic waste …
Do you have water-efficient faucets in your home?
I have no idea!
I suppose I could try flexitarianism. I could be a vegetarian half the week.
That's a good idea. Vegetarianism is more animal-friendly and environment-friendly, too!
I do what I can, but it doesn't feel like it's changing anything.
Yeah, but we have to start somewhere. The real problem is education.

Talking about duration

Unit 2
I have been walking to work once a week.
I have been studying English all weekend.
Guess what! I go to the gym twice a week now.

Phrase Bank

Really? How long have you been going there?
Are you reading anything now?
Yeah, I'm reading a graded reader.
How long have you been reading it?
She's been trying a new superfood. It's made her feel much better.
I collect old vinyl pop records.
No way! How long have you been collecting them?
Well, it all started when …

The environment

Unit 2
I feel a bit more optimistic about threatened species because there are lots of conservation groups trying to stop extinction.
I think the scientist who makes the first point will say climate change is also a problem right now.
Floods are a real problem in São Paulo.
And it's gotten worse recently.
I can't believe there are only about 800 gorillas left!
It makes me want to do something.
Me, too. I think it's actually worse. I heard recently we've lost more than half the world's wildlife since 1970!
We should be taught more about it at school.
I've been trying to walk more instead of driving everywhere.
Good for you. I should use my car less.
I think using hybrid cars will make a big difference.

Describing places

Unit 3
These two look like fashionable neighborhoods …
There's a bridge in this one.
I'd say our city is chaotic. There's lots of traffic and millions of people.
We have a beautiful square in the heart of our town. It's a real tourist spot because it has great cafés and restaurants.
A dangerous, ancient, Asian, skyscraper.
The city I'd like to visit has beautiful beaches, great music, and some of the best colonial architecture in South America. It's well-known for its mix of European, African, and indigenous cultures. Famous landmarks include …
Last year I went to this amazing place. I'd never been before, and to my surprise, it was completely empty. I'd expected it to be full!
I saw the pyramids in Egypt five years ago. I'd never seen anything so old before!
My home town, Trujillo, has some great colonial architecture.

Urban problems

Unit 3
I think the worst problem by far is the traffic.
No way! I'd say vandalism is a much more serious issue.
Littering bothers me a lot.
The traffic doesn't bother me..
In my neighborhood, there is trash everywhere.
All the traffic jams drive me crazy!

Making guesses and deductions

Unit 5
I think he must be talking to his son.
Hmm … Not sure. I think he might be talking to a friend.
I think the first one might be true, but I'm not really sure.
Really? I actually think it could be bad for your teeth.
You look in shape. I think you might work out a lot in your free time.
Yeah, I saw you carrying a tennis racket the other day. You must play tennis.
I'd say it's probably about consumer behavior.

Reinforcing

Unit 3
I'm afraid so.
I'm afraid not.

Apologizing

Unit 3
I'm sorry. I didn't realize that.

School life

Unit 4
All the books remind me of my school bag. It was really heavy!
I used to hate math because the teacher couldn't explain it to us.
Maybe they have a lot of expensive private schools.
Yes, I guess the teachers are well qualified, too.
They have one-on-one tutoring sometimes. We don't get that if we fail a test.
It'd be a nice modern building. We would only do a little homework every day and not take a lot of tests. And I think uniforms are a good idea.
No way! I love wearing my own clothes.
At my school, students have too much homework. It takes me four or five hours a day.
Well, when I was in high school, I had a lot of homework, too.
I think too much pressure can be very stressful for students
You're absolutely right, but if there isn't enough competition, students can get lazy.

Picking a career

Unit 4
Yes, me! I tried three completely different jobs until I found the right one for me.
Really? What did you do?
I can't throw away $40,000, drop out of college, forget about my business major and start over.
I'd love to get a scholarship to go to Harvard, but it's so hard I won't even try.
All my friends will major in business, so that's what I'll do.
My parents have always wanted me to get into medical school. I can't disappoint them, and they are desperate for me to succeed.

Phrase Bank

I'd love to get a degree in music, but what will I do when I graduate? How will I get a decent job?
I have all the education I need, I'm not illiterate! It's time for fun, fun, fun!

Should have
Unit 4
I should have studied English when I was a kid.
I should have thought about it more carefully.
I shouldn't have listened to him.
What should I have studied instead?
You should have studied harder for the test.
I shouldn't have missed so many classes.
Me, too. I should have participated more.
They should have stayed at home.
I shouldn't have told my sister I didn't like her new dress.

First and second conditional
Unit 4
If I have time, I'll come and visit you.
If you could travel anywhere in the world, where would you go?
If I get my driving license soon, I'll be able to get a better job.
What kind of job would you get if you passed your test?
If I'd had more confidence, I would have sung at the karaoke competition.
Do you think you'd have won?

Third conditional
Unit 5
If she hadn't gone to college, she might'nt have gotten into debt.
If I hadn't played so many video games, I'd have been better at sport!
Which sports would you have played?
I'd volunteer to help with reading at my local elementary school.
I think some parents would donate to V2Z.

Criticizing
Unit 4
Will you ever learn?
You should have known better.
How could you do such a thing?
What were you thinking?

Expressing sympathy
Unit 4
It could have been worse.
Don't let it get you down.
What's done is done.
It's not the end of the world.

Shopping
Unit 5
I expect good customer service.
Yes, and I like it to be well organized, so I can find things easily.
Well, they probably all shop online and don't go to real stores anymore.
I agree with a lot of it, but I still prefer to buy things online. It's so much easier.
No way, what for? Who would care about my shopping?
There's no need to stand in in that long line. They have self-checkout here.
My battery is running out. Are there charging stations in here?
Smart brands use customers' user-generated content, such as YouTube videos and blog posts, to advertise their products.
I would rather do in-store shopping than shop online. At least you can try things on.
I've got a discount for that store—you get 10% off everything today.
I can't get online to check the reviews. They don't even have free Wi-Fi in here!
These glasses looked good on me with virtual try-on, but they don't look good in real life.
I don't have much brand loyalty except for my cell phone—I'd never consider getting any other make.
I guess I'm 4 for most things except clothes. I like to try things on before buying.
It could be good for clothes hoarders.
Yeah, they could sell clothes they haven't worn.

Talking about products
Unit 5
I bought some really expensive sunglasses and left them in a taxi. I felt really guilty afterward – and stupid, too.
I bought it on impulse. It was pure madness!
It seemed like a wonderful product, but it was such a disappointment.
They go on and on in the infomercial about how it's natural.
I guess it's just so fashionable these days.
I like to wear dark colours, especially at night.
Not me. I'm into bright shirts or T-shirts.

Shopping problems
Unit 5
Do you have a size ten in stock?
I'm sorry ma'am, we're sold out.
Ah, that's a shame. It seems impossible to find larger sizes.
Can you email me when you have some in stock?
Ah. I'm afraid your card has been declined.
Declined! I don't understand! It's a new card, and I know I'm not over my limit. There must be a problem with your card machine.
I'd like to return this phone. I bought it here the other day and it's damaged.
Well, uh, unfortunately we can't give you a refund, but we'd be happy to exchange it for another one.
Sure, uh, I just need to see your receipt.

Phrase Bank

Other useful expressions

Unit 1
I guess one advantage is that you get to know a lot of different people.
Neither of us has a nickname.

Unit 3
My parents never used to pick up after their dog, but now they always do.

TV

Unit 6
I don't watch a lot of TV, but I sometimes watch …
That's not me at all. I'm really into …
People can watch TV outside the house now.
Yes, and my parents didn't use to have a remote control to change channels.
Well, these days you can subscribe to lots of different services, so we have a lot more options.
True, but there are too many options sometimes.
I sometimes watch English language programs with subtitles to practice my English.

Describing people

Unit 6
She's not really my thing.
She's an American TV host who interviews famous people.
I've seen Joaquin Phoenix in a few interviews. He's really rude, which is embarrassing for the talk-show host.

Giving opinions

Unit 6
I was totally addicted to *How I Met Your Mother* a few years ago.
I loved the first episode of *Mad Men*. It was so stylish!
I didn't use to like them to be honest. I thought they were weird.
"Despacito" is a very catchy song.
The music in that movie is great.
I've seen lots of "Harlem Shake" videos. My class made one and uploaded it.
Really? I didn't like them to be honest. I thought they were weird.

Unit 7
I think they're becoming less and less interested in foreign affairs.
I think the weakest arguments are the ones about Tom's son. I mean, who cares?
I think it's awful to say young people are ignorant. Of course we're not!
I know! We have access to so much information. How can we be ignorant?
I'd never read that book. I mean, life's too short.
Don't trust anyone under 30? Come on!
We can't deny that …
Hold on a second, let me finish.

Well, it depends on what you mean by reading.
That may be true, but don't you think …?
Well, you may agree or disagree, but he makes some valid points.
Yeah, I couldn't agree more.
My point exactly! I totally disagree.

Unit 9
I think all of them were pretty stupid, but the guy who showed his ID was the worst.
That's why I really think songs, books and music should be completely free.

Making deductions

Unit 7
I think the first one could be a piano.
Maybe. Or a cell phone. That would make sense.
It seems to me that our teenagers are a bit different.

Unit 8
Maybe there was a metal pole in his jacket.
I don't think so. Maybe he was attached to wires.
The driver might've put his wallet on the car roof when he was opening the door.
And then he must have forgotten about it and started driving. What do you think?
I imagine the first one probably belongs to a woman because …

Unit 9
First one … Well, let's see. Maybe he left his driver's license at the store and went back to get it?
I think the burglar is going to say he entered the wrong house.
Maybe they're … waiting to meet …

Expressing surprise

Unit 6
What? Get out of here!
Really? You're kidding, right?
No way! You mean your sister actually met Emma Stone?
My goodness!
Are you serious?
That can't be true. I don't believe you.

Unit 7
Oh, yeah? How come?

Talking about technology

Unit 7
No, I guess I'm just lucky when I buy things.
I heard something about a virus that made private social media information become public.
I guess it'll say we can check anything on our phones.
And to be careful about fake news!
There are too many choices now. It was easier to focus before.

Phrase Bank

Effortless? No way! It takes ages to learn to use technology well!
Yes, and people had better memories. You don't have to remember anything anymore. Your phone knows everything.
Do you know any good apps that can help you pick up a language?
Yes, there are lots! Duolingo is a good one.
I love Evernote Scannable! You just zoom into the document or card or whatever, and the app converts it into a scan. Then you can just scroll through all of your saved documents.
I'm not sure. It could be a vacuum cleaner.
Stephen Hawking used a cheek-controlled communication system.
And this meant he could speak through a computer.
I use it a lot. I can tell it who to call.
I only use it to choose songs to play.
My GPS is voice-activated, but it's kind of stupid.
Oh, yes, you can mount it on the wall yourself.
It works just as well as the famous brand, but it's half the price.
You'll be able to use it in any country, don't worry.
Some of the keys are different, but it's basically the same thing.

Unit 9
I try to create really difficult passwords.

Indirect questions

Unit 7
Excuse me, could you tell me where the station is?
Do you know where he went?
Could you tell me whether it could work in any car?
Do you know if people with disabilities would be able to use it?

Reporting

Unit 7
The salesman said some of the keys were different.
He said that it worked just as well as the famous brand.
The delivery guy told me I could mount it on the wall myself.
On the site it said I'd be able to use it in any country.
The store manager said it had just arrived.

Photography and photographs

Unit 8
I use Photoshop to remove unncessary objects from my photos – like trash cans!
I've never used it. I like my photos to show reality.
Well, I guess it depends how you use it. If you work in the advertising industry, then it has had a positive influence.
Look at this one. It looks like the giraffe is photobombing them!
The caption could be, "I'm much better looking than him!"

She disappears when someone tries to take a photo. She's incredibly camera-shy.
Retouching your vacation photos to make the weather look better is really easy!
This flash should reduce red-eye.
The court discovered that the prosecution had doctored the image.
The photographer managed to get a candid picture of the princess laughing.
The picture on the front cover had been photoshopped to make him look muscular.
Did you see that great photo from the Oscars a few years ago? Even celebrities are into this photobombing craze.

Speculating about the past

Unit 8
The tickets must have been very expensive.
He can't have known my date of birth.
I don't know how he did that trick. He must have had the ring in a secret pocket.
He can't have levitated.
He might have practiced enough.
It can't have been comfortable in that block of ice.

Unit 9
Hmm … I don't know. It might've been a mistake.

Actions / services other people do for you

Unit 8
We still need to have the cake made.
We're going to have a new suit made.
I got my nails done, too.
Did you have it dyed?
Really? I don't know how to. I'd have to get it fixed.
I can't stand my living room The paint is a horrible color. I'm going to have it repainted one of these days.

Expressing preferences

Unit 8
I prefer Ray-Ban. Their designs are cooler.
I love this class. It's really interesting.
Which one do you like better?
Both are OK, I guess.
I think I like the old one better than the new one.
I don't really like either of them.
I actually prefer the second one to the first.

Tag questions

Unit 8
You really like baseball, don't you?
You haven't done anything crazy, have you?
It's great, isn't it?
He'll love it, won't he?
You didn't do it all yourself, did you?
That rug wasn't there before, was it?
You know he's going to be over the moon, don't you?

Phrase Bank

Crime and punishment

Unit 9
To me, credit-card fraud is the least serious crime.
Well, it depends on the amount of money you steal, doesn't it?
Most students, four out of five actually, think credit-card fraud has increased.
The crime everybody I asked would eliminate forever is …
I think the bank robber should be sentenced to at least five years.
No, that's not fair. I mean, what if she dies in prison?

Talking about the future

Unit 9
By 2025, cyber attacks will have become the world's top threat.
He'll be telling us if we should take these warnings seriously.
Cybercriminals will be carrying out attacks wirelessly, and we won't be protected.
They will have developed the ability to spread viruses across multiple devices very, very easily.
Cybercriminals will have targeted 20 percent of all the world's smart phones …
I won't be working in ten years, I'll have retired.
It's possible we'll all be driving electric cars by 2030.
Really? I doubt that very much. I think lots of people will have stopped driving completely.

Giving excuses

Unit 9
This is not what it looks like!
Just hear me out!
It's not what you're thinking.
It's not what it seems.
Hold on! I can explain.

Moods

Unit 10
I'm not convinced it's all true. I don't think that "nothing can upset me"!
You mean you're never grumpy? What's your secret?
Life is short, and I'm just happy to be alive!
Carlos reminds me of my brother. A bit grumpy!
I definitely have my ups and downs, but I'm usually in a better mood in winter, when it's cooler.
Not me. I'm much more emotional than that.
No, I don't have pet peeves. I'm cool as a cucumber!
Yes! When someone talks during a film and then asks, "Who's he?" "What happened?" etc.
People who change the TV channel without asking.
Yeah, and taxi drivers who know keep talking about themselves!
I'm sick and tired of …

Learning English

Unit 10
Let's see … First one … I agree. I think I'm good at grammar.
I'm not. I'm good at listening, but I'm really bad at grammar.
I'm OK with grammar—especially verb tenses. But I find pronunciation hard, like the "th" sound.

Making recommendations

Unit 10
To practice listening, watch TV first without subtitles, then again with subtitles to check.
Try to focus on expressing your ideas fluently.
A good way of practicing is watching Internet videos.
You should consider giving pronunciation a little more attention.
Try to avoid reading slowly all the time.
How about learning "make an effort" instead of "effort"?
Have you thought about using a pronunciation book with audio to practice? Or finding some pronunciation videos on YouTube?

Other useful expressions

Unit 6
Well, I guess it's important to get permission to film in some places.
Yes, she offered to share her cab from the airport
I think she asked Sia why she wears a wig like that.
Well, I'd like to ask her where she gets her inspiration from.
I love James Corden's Carpool Karaoke, where he sings with musicians. Have you see any of them? He actually did a great one with Sia!

Unit 7
OK, so he said "cat," but he meant "car." I guess "blood" could be …
They might say a color looks great on you when it really doesn't!

Unit 8
I'd probably fix a broken faucet myself.
I like to have a special meal out, blow out my candles, then go dancing.
I was an only child, so yeah, my mom spoiled me a lot.

Unit 9
Hey, what do you think you're doing?

Unit 10
Mario, welcome to the group. What brings you here?
Yeah, I think so. A friend of mine took a course like this once.

Word List

This is a reference list. To check pronunciation of any individual words, you can use a talking dictionary.

Unit 1

Relationships
to be attracted to someone
to break up
to drift apart
to fall for someone
to fall out with someone
to get along (well)
to get (back) together
to get to know someone (better)
to hang out
to move in

Personality adjectives
adventure-seeking
confident
easygoing
fun-loving
funny
honest
impolite
kind-hearted
knowledgeable
like-minded
open-minded
outgoing
self-centered
shy
sociable
thoughtful

Unit 2

Going green
appliances
bottled water
carbon footprint
disposable products
eco-friendly
energy-efficient light bulb
environment-friendly appliances
faucet
household waste
insecticides
nature-friendly
plastic bags
public transportation
recycled paper
refillable bottles
renewable energy
reusable cloth bag
solar heating
Styrofoam cup
vegan

The environment
climate change
deforestation
droughts
dumping
floods
fossil fuels

global warming
poaching
rising sea levels
threatened species

Threatened species
Giant panda
Golden lion tamarin
Ivory-billed woodpecker
Javanese rhino
Monk seal
Mountain gorilla
North Atlantic right whale

Unit 3

Cities
harbor
landmark
neighborhood
skyline
skyscraper
smog
square

Adjectives
chaotic
dangerous
exceptional
fashionable
flat
lively
magnificent
marvellous
rundown
ugly
upscale

Social conventions and manners
to blow your nose in public
to blow on your soup
to bow
to chew
to hug
to kiss on the cheek
to leave a tip
to push your way through the crowd
to shake hands

Urban problems
crime rate
debt lines
littering
loneliness
noise pollution
pickpocketing
parking spot
potholes
roadwork
security checks
theft / thieves
to go through red lights
to honk

traffic jams
trash
vandalism
work-life balance

Rules and regulations
fine
lifeguard
on duty
to fasten
to pick up after
to refrain from
to tow away
trespasser
under surveillance

Unit 4

School life
badly paid teachers
career counseling
discipline problems
extracurricular activities
one-on-one tutoring
overcrowded classrooms
pressure
report card
schedule
subjects
to behave badly
to cheat on exams
to do the homework
to do well (in school)
to fail a test
to get a low / high grade
to get kicked out of class
to make mistakes
to take a class / tests
tuition fees

College life
certificate
degree
graduate
major (in)
scholarship
to drop out of college
to enroll
to get into (medical) school
to start over

Other words
autism
deadline
gifted
illiterate
IQ (intelligence quotient)
jigsaw
learning disability
to learn by heart
to skip
trouble sleeping
volume

Unit 5

Money and shopping
brand loyalty
charging stations
discount code
self-checkout
shop online
shopping sprees
to do in-store shopping
to save money
user-generated content
virtual try-on

Word formation
actually
apparently
appearance
comfortable
convenience
currently
enjoyment
fitness
flatten
freaky
generalize
gorgeous
remarkable
seriously
shockingly
solution
tighten
useless

Other words
aisles
checkout
gadgets
lucrative
to donate
to get into debt

Unit 6

TV genres and expressions
cartoons
cooking programs
documentaries
dubbed
game shows
medical drama
music programs
news programs
reality TV
reviews
season
sitcoms
soap operas
sports events
stand-up comedy
subtitles
talk shows
to be addicted to

Word List

to subscribe to
trailer
wildlife programs

Movies and videos

best-selling
blockbuster
cast
clips
prequel
role
script
sequel
to be nominated
to be set in
to shoot
to star
trilogy

Other words

accent
composer
renowned
views

Unit 7

Phrasal verbs

break into
calm down
cut down on
find out
go on
pick up
set up
take out

Using touch screens

to double tap
to drag and drop
to scroll
to swipe
to zoom

Other words

break down
bugs
carrier
launch
warranty

Unit 8

Photoshop

camera-shy
candid photo
red-eye
to doctor images
to photobomb
to photoshop

Furniture

bedside table
bookcase
chair

closet
comforter
double bed
dresser
blanket
lamp
mirror
pillow
rug
wall
window

Opinion essays

Although / Even though / Though
Consequently
Despite / In spite of
For instance
In addition to that
It is usually said that
On the one hand
On the other hand
To sum up

Unit 9

Crime and punishment

acquit
be arrested
bribery
burglary
charge with
convict
credit card fraud
domestic abuse
drug dealing
fine
kidnapping
murder
(music) piracy
release
robbery
send to jail
sentence (to)
take to court
tax evasion
theft

Careers for the future

3D printing engineers
book-to-app converters
nano-medics
privacy manager
turbine specialist

Other words

captive
carry out
gang
shoot
spread
targeted
taxpayer
threat
warnings

Unit 10

Moods

cool as a cucumber
grumpy
moody
pet peeves
short-tempered
to be in a good mood
to bite your nails
to get fed up with
to swear
to yell at

Binomials

again and again
little by little
peace and quiet
sick and tired
sooner or later
ups and downs

Phrasal verbs

to boss sb around
to bring sb down
to come down with sth
to cut down on
to figure sth out
to lift sb up
to look for sth
to put off sth
to stick to sth

Other words

can't stand
critical
emotional support
payback plan
tough

Verbs

Irregular verbs

Irregular verbs can be difficult to remember. Try remembering them in groups with similar sounds, conjugation patterns, or spellings.

Simple past and Past participle are the same

Base form	Simple past	Past participle
bring	brought /brɔt/	brought
buy	bought	bought
catch	caught /cɔt/	caught
fight	fought	fought
teach	taught	taught
think	thought	thought
feed	fed	fed
feel	felt	felt
keep	kept	kept
leave	left	left
mean	meant /mɛnt/	meant
meet	met	met
sleep	slept	slept
lay	laid	laid
pay	paid	paid
sell	sold	sold
tell	told	told
send	sent	sent
spend	spent	spent
stand	stood /stʊd/	stood
understand	understood	understood
lose	lost	lost
shoot	shot	shot
can	could	could
will	would	would
build	built /bɪlt/	built
find	found /faʊnd/	found
hang	hung	hung
have	had	had
hear	heard /hɜrd/	heard
hold	held	held
make	made	made
say	said /sɛd/	said
sit	sat	sat
swing	swung /swʌŋ/	swung
win	won /wʌn/	won

Base form and Past participle are the same

Base form	Simple past	Past participle
become	became	become
come	came	come
run	ran	run

No changes across the three forms

Base form	Simple past	Past participle
cost	cost	cost
cut	cut	cut
hit	hit	hit
let	let	let
put	put /pʊt/	put
quit	quit /kwɪt/	quit
set	set	set
split	split	split

Special cases

Base form	Simple past	Past participle
be	was / were	been
draw	drew /druː/	drawn /drɔn/
fly	flew /fluː/	flown /floʊn/
lie	lay	lain
read	read /rɛd/	read /rɛd/

Simple past + -en

Base form	Simple past	Past participle
beat	beat	beaten
bite	bit	bitten
break	broke	broken
choose	chose	chosen
forget	forgot	forgotten
freeze	froze	frozen
get	got	got / gotten
speak	spoke	spoken
steal	stole	stolen
wake	woke	woken

Verbs

Simple past + -en

Base form	Simple past	Past participle
beat	beat	beaten
bite	bit	bitten
break	broke	broken
choose	chose	chosen
forget	forgot	forgotten
freeze	froze	frozen
get	got	got / gotten
speak	spoke	spoken
steal	stole	stolen
wake	woke	woken

Base form + -en

Base form	Simple past	Past participle
drive	drove	driven /drɪvən/
eat	ate	eaten
fall	fell	fallen
give	gave	given
ride	rode	ridden /rɪdən/
see	saw /sɔ/	seen
shake	shook	shaken
take	took	taken
write	wrote	written /rɪtən/

Base form ending in o + -ne

Base form	Simple past	Past participle
do	did	done /dʌn/
go	went	gone /gɔn/

i - a - u

Base form	Simple past	Past participle
begin	began	begun
drink	drank	drunk
ring	rang	rung
sing	sang	sung
swim	swam	swum

ow - ew - own

Base form	Simple past	Past participle
blow	blew /bluː/	blown
grow	grew	grown
know	knew	known
throw	threw	thrown

ear - ore - orn

Base form	Simple past	Past participle
swear	swore	sworn
tear /tɛr/	tore	torn
wear	wore	worn

Common stative verbs

Thinking / opinions

(dis)agree	imagine	realize	suppose
believe	know	recognize	think
depend	matter	remember	understand
guess	mean	seem	

Feelings / emotions

feel (=have an opinion)	(dis)like love	prefer promise	wish
hate	need	want	

Senses

see	taste	feel
hear	smell	

Others

belong	have	involve
contain	include	own

Use stative verbs:

▸ to describe states / opinions, not actions.
I believe in God. I hate spiders.
▸ in the simple form, even for temporary situations.
Sorry, we don't understand. NOT ~~We aren't understanding.~~

Note:

▸ Some verbs which are usually stative can be actions:
I think that's a good idea. (opinion).
It's lunchtime, so I'm thinking about food. (action)
We're having a 10-minute break.
▸ A few, especially *like* and *love* are increasingly used in speech as "actions":
I'm liking this burger.
I've been loving you for so long …

79

Richmond

58 St Aldates
Oxford
OX1 1ST
United Kingdom

ISBN: 978-84-668-3056-0
Fourth reprint: 2022
CP: 944443
© Richmond / Santillana Global S.L. 2019

All rights reserved. No part of this book may be reproduced, stored in a retrieval system or transmitted in any form by any means, electronic, mechanical, photocopying, recording or otherwise, without the prior permission in writing of the Publisher.

Publishing Director: Deborah Tricker
Publishers: Luke Baxter, Laura Miranda
Media Publisher: Luke Baxter
Content development: José Luiz Morales, Angie Vasconcellos, Ricardo Sili, Tom Abraham, Damian Williams
Editors: Helen Wendholt
Proofreaders: Lily Khambata, Diyan Leake, Rachael Williamson
Design Manager: Lorna Heaslip
Cover Design: Lorna Heaslip
Design & Layout: Dave Kuzmicki
Photo Researcher: Magdalena Mayo
Audio Production: John Marshall Media Inc.

We would like to thank all those who have given their kind permission to reproduce material for this book:

Illustrators: Alexandre Matos, Rico

Photos:
ALAMY/Zoonar GmbH, PictureLux / The Hollywood Archive, imageBROKER / Alamy Stock Photo, Jeffrey Blackler; GETTY IMAGES SALES SPAIN/Kati1313, Pidjoe, Bmcent1, Tim Hawley, Sam Edwards, LordRunar, Maskot, Ridofranz, Wavebreak, Westend61, RobHoglund, RugliG, Popperfoto, SensorSpot, Jacobs Stock Photography Ltd, Graiki, LittleBee80, 10'000 Hours, Giuilio Fornasar, Paul Quayle, Aldo Murillo, Ethan Miller, Luis Alvarez, Caspar Benson, Klaus Vedfelt, Siri Stafford, Wavebreakmedia, Yuricazac, William Perugini, Betsie Van der Meer, Jose Luiz Pelaez Inc, Monkey Business Images, High Street Studios LLC, Maria Taglienti-Molinari, Portra, Tetra Images - Jessica Peterson, JohnnyGreig; SHUTTERSTOCK/ Rovio/Columbia/Sony Animation/Village Roadshow/Kobal/ Shutterstock, ZQFotography, Preto Perola, Levent Konuk, A SDF_ MEDIA, gorbelabda, iQuoncept, Poznyakov, Gravicapa, file404; ARCHIVO SANTILLANA

Podcast / Video: My Damn Channel; Geobeats

The Publisher has made every effort to trace the owner of copyright material; however, the Publisher will correct any involuntary omission at the earliest opportunity.

Printed in Brazil by Forma Certa Gráfica Digital
Lote: 808128
Codigo: 290530560 / 2025